MAN BUILDS TOMORROW ... In Today's World

In Today's World Series

Etta Schneider Ress, Ed. D., *editor*

CITIES AND METROPOLITAN AREAS
Samuel L. Arbital

MAN AND HIS RESOURCES
C. W. Mattison
Joseph Alvarez

MAN BUILDS TOMORROW
Etta Schneider Ress
Gina Liebow

SIGNALS TO SATELLITES
Etta Schneider Ress

TRANSPORTATION
Etta Schneider Ress

MAN BUILDS TOMORROW

....In Today's World

by

Etta Schneider Ress

Gina Liebow

in collaboration with

John Christianson and
I. I. Olicker

Published by

CREATIVE
EDUCATIONAL
SOCIETY, INC.

Mankato, Minnesota

Contents

CHAPTER 1   MAN AND HIS CULTURE

CHAPTER 2   MAN AND HIS WORK

CHAPTER 3   AUTOMATION: A NEW LOOK AT MAN AND HIS WORK

CHAPTER 4   EDUCATION IN THE AMERICAN TRADITION

CHAPTER 5   EACH HUMAN BEING — A VALUABLE RESOURCE

CHAPTER 6   HUMAN RESOURCES AROUND THE GLOBE

Man the explorer, the producer, active
participant in the community. Sculpture
by Alexander Calder for the 1967 Mon-
treal World Exposition on **Man and His
World.**

6

Preface

BUILDING TOMORROW: *Past, Present and Future*

Why is our nation engaged in a program of great vision to raise the expectations and achievements of all people in our own country and, to the best of our ability, in countries around the world? How will tomorrow differ from today in extending the benefits of science and technology? How much of the present do we owe to the past?

MAN BUILDS TOMORROW . . . IN TODAY'S WORLD is an attempt to relate the present with the past, to show through words and photographs how the hard work of millions of people over thousands of years, guided by the daring and imagination of creative minds, built a civilization in which most people living today can share.

The American people are a blend of many cultures, each with enough likeness and difference to contribute to a great productive nation. They built a democratic nation where farmers, loggers, workers in factory, office, and the professions, together with businessmen and statesmen, benefit from a high standard of living. It would appear that the dream of our ancestors for a great society has been realized — almost, but not quite. For, there are still millions of men, women, and children throughout the land who do not share in our prosperity, many of whom have untapped creative talents.

And so, a bold and imaginative plan is under way — to provide better educational and economic opportunity for all and thus erase poverty, unemployment, ignorance, slums, and ill health. Some of the plans for human betterment are described in the book. From these plans may come a greater society and a greater nation. The challenge and the opportunity belong to today's youth.

Digital Equipment Corp.

CHAPTER 1

MAN AND HIS CULTURE

Man himself is mankind's greatest resource. Man has walked this earth for a million years and more. His eyes look forward, not off to the sides like fish eyes, and he perceives depth. He can see sizes and forms, and most men also see colors, not just shades of gray. Man walks upright. His hands are free. These hands are wonderfully formed to grasp, push, seize, hold, twist, and manipulate in a thousand ways. His brain is large. His power is so great that he rules the world, lording over the animals, transforming deserts into farmlands, islands into cities, rocky ores into polished metals, wood pulp into books. Only man can do these things. He is his own greatest resource.

Man's power comes from culture, not muscles and fangs. Culture characterizes humanity. It depends upon man's large brain and his ability to think. Culture consists of the things that are learned and passed on by human beings — speech, beliefs, customs, laws, religion, technology, all traditions and knowledge.

Men must live together to have a culture. The ancient Greek philosopher, Aristotle, realized this and summed it up in a simple sentence, "Man is a social animal," and so man has been since earliest times.

During those millions of years, human beings have been living together, learning, teaching, improving upon the learnings of others — building human culture. For most of that time, cultural change was almost unbelievably slow. People achieved a pattern of life which kept them alive; this pattern they passed on to their children. Mere survival was a major factor in human life, as it is today among some tribes of people in remote places. For many thousands of years, man's tools consisted of stones. Man remained a hunter, a fisher, a gatherer of fruits and berries, a grubber of wild roots. Men probably grunted and passed on what they knew from one generation to the next. That was in the long age known as the Old Stone Age.

But did these earliest men have a language, or did they teach by grunting and showing? Did they have beliefs of any kind, customs, superstitions? Did they have any tools besides hunks of rock, made of perishable materials, such as wooden clubs, cords of vines, or animal skins? These are questions we cannot answer at present. All we know is that they were like a bunch of smart apes, not much more complex. Their physical resources were not much better than those of apes.

Yet they had a culture. They lived together, they learned things and taught others what they had learned. They had a tradition. We recognize them as human beings.

American Museum of Nat. Hist.

In Africa, archaeologists have unearthed the bones and remains of the earliest known man. He was a creature they call Australopithecus africanus. He stood about five feet tall, had a heavy ridge of bone above his deepset eyes, his forehead sloped backwards, his heavy jaw stuck out, but without a chin, like an ape's jaw. He lived in open, arid country and ate anything he could get his hands on — roots, plants, animal meat. A similar creature, Australopithecus robustus, lived in the wet forests and was mainly a vegetarian.

These creatures are the earliest men yet discovered. They had a brain about the size of a modern ape's brain. They lived a million, possibly as much as 1,700,000 years ago.

We know very little about them or their culture — only what we can learn from fragmentary material remains. We know that they lived together, learned to use simple tools, and taught others of their kind to use the same tools. They learned to pick up rocks and throw them at their prey. They took hard rocks and whacked away until they chipped out a sharp edge, then they used these rocks as tools for cutting and skinning. No doubt they also had special ways of hunting which they learned and passed on and knew which plants were poisonous and which were edible.

The Stone Age way of life still serves several tribes of people in Australia and Africa. For them, cultural change has been very slow and they survive by hunting and gathering fruits, living always at the edge of starvation and disease. Turn to page 136 for a view of some of these people who have been able to leap the hurdle of centuries with the aid of adequate food, homes, and education.

In Denmark, archaeologists found the fragments of a prehistoric fish-trap, shown here. It was woven of birch twigs about 5,000 years ago, around the end of the Paleolithic period. It has been preserved by lying under water. In the many generations since then, Danish fishermen have continued to prepare traps in the same way, using the same kind of materials. Thus have the generations of men been able to keep a line of communication open without a break.

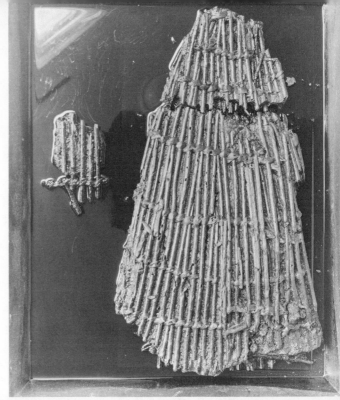

Danish National Museum

Australian News Bureau

Civilization Develops

Human culture was not entirely static during the Paleolithic period. Gradually, very gradually, human traditions grew more complex. Speech patterns developed into language, and language made it much easier to pass on patterns of culture from one generation to the next. Language is mankind's most important and distinctive tool. It allows men to think, react, learn, teach, and live like human beings. Without language, each generation would start out and end up like animals — or at the very best, like cave men — because it would be impossible to pass on knowledge and thus make cultural progress. The development of human culture itself and all utilization of our human resources depends upon language.

Early people also learned to use fire, they skinned a n i m a l s and chewed the hides to make them soft, they made bone into fishhooks and needles, they developed new techniques for chipping hard flint into graceful daggers and scythes. They learned to braid hair into ropes and belts, weave reeds into baskets and fishtraps, make clay into pottery, string a bow and shoot arrows.

Over the long centuries, man evolved physically from a sulking, bony-browed brute into a specimen no different from ourselves. He grew tall and straight; his brain grew large.

Throughout the long Paleolithic millennia, most human life was nomadic. Tribes of hunters wandered about like the beasts following herds of reindeer, seeking the wild oxen and boars of the forest, ducks and geese in the marshes, antelope on the steppes; picking berries, fruits and grasses in season; migrating northwards in the summer, or up into the mountains, then down again to escape the cold of winter; living in caves or crude huts or under the stars.

Pekin people in China used fire during the Old Stone Age.

Artist's view of Cro-Magnon life.

Sometimes fishermen stayed in small villages along shallow waters, sucking oysters and eating fish all their life long.

In the later Paleolithic period, skilled flintsmiths sometimes became specialists, wandering about trading sharp daggers, axes, arrowpoints, and scythes for the things they needed to survive. Other men became specialists in magic — witch doctors and shamans. But most of the people moved about, always in small family packs, hunting. For all of them life was hard and short, though some, like the Cro-Magnon men of southern Europe, became skilled artists and hunters. But few men used their human resources to outwit nature, since control of nature was beyond them.

These early people came to fear the dead and have ideas of a life after death. They learned to draw pictures and carve images, use magic to bewitch and kill animals and cure the sick. They learned these and many other things. From man to man, they handed on what they knew. Over these thousands of years, human culture gradually grew more complex.

Cave drawings of Stone Age people in Spain resemble those of present-day Bushmen in Africa and tribes in Australia.

13

Agriculture Begins

Man, the hunter, had been skillful, slyer than the fox, stronger than the bear, armed with weapons and sustained by a hunter's culture. Man lived as a wandering hunter for thousands of years. Then came a revolution, some 7,000 years ago. It transformed the conditions of human life and expanded human resources far beyond those of hunters and savages.

This was the Neolithic Revolution, the coming of agriculture. It began in the hill country around the Fertile Crescent, site of modern Iran, Iraq, Syria and Israel. Here the hills circle around the broad valley of the Tigris and Euphrates Rivers, then roll on down towards Sinai and the valley of the Nile. In these hills lived hunters and gatherers. They were the first men to catch and tame animals. They were the first to plant grasses and raise grains.

At the place called Jarmo in Iraq, archaeologists have unearthed the site of a village which existed for about three hundred years up to around 5000 B.C. The people lived in huts of sun-dried clay. Two kinds of wheat and barley were found among the ruins of their village. So were the bones of sheep, goats, pigs, and cattle. Many tools were found, together with pottery, obsidian from Turkey, and little clay figurines of fat women — probably images of the bountiful earth mother, the farmers' goddess. The Jarmo people, with their grain fields and domesticated animals, lived by agriculture.

From the Fertile Crescent, farmers carried agriculture to the far corners of the Old World and even beyond. They brought along their domesticated strains of the plants and animals that are still found in the hills and valleys of the Fertile Crescent — barley and wheat, dogs, cattle, sheep, goats, pigs, and horses. In some places local animals were domesticated and added to the local livestock, among them elephants, camels, reindeer, and cats. In other places there were independent discoveries of agriculture, such as in China, where men began to cultivate millet and rice, or in Central America, where they discovered how to raise corn, squash, and beans.

These first farmers throughout the world still used tools of stone, or else of wood, leather, and bone. They still lived in the Stone Age. But their way of life was so different from that of hunters, that we speak now of the Neolithic or New Stone Age, the age of the farmer.

Sickle blades found at Jarmo.

Oriental Institute by Robert Braidwood

Excavation of part of Jarmo, a farming community.

Am. Museum Nat. Hist.

Diorama of a village in Denmark about 5,000 years ago.

15

River Valley Peoples: The Sumerians

Agriculture allowed men to live in larger groups, and it allowed them to settle down. Agriculture could feed many more mouths than hunting; the human population increased rapidly. Thus the Neolithic Revolution brought history's first population explosion. At the same time, huts and caves gave way to buildings of brick and stone. Settlements grew larger and larger.

By around the year 4000 B.C., hill country farmers had come down into the lowlands in the valley of the Tigris and Euphrates Rivers. For awhile, they lived as they had before. Then they built dams to control the violent rivers, and canals to use the waters for irrigating fields. They brought forth bounteous crops from the rich valley soil. Their villages

University Museum, U. of Penn.

Site of Ur. Sumerian city mentioned in the Bible.

Fertile Crescent Area.

From **The Great Adventure** by Hunnicutt and Grambs. Reproduced with permission, L. W. Singer Co.

Reconstruction of a battle in the walled city of Ur.

grew into cities. Their culture became civilization.

Civilization is an advanced state of human culture. It goes beyond the culture of wandering hunters or isolated fish eaters, even beyond that of hill country farmers like the people of Jarmo. First, agriculture allows the human population to multiply. When it also allows a few men to feed many, so that a multitude of new human occupations can come about, then we speak of civilization. The word comes from Latin *civitas,* which means "city." Civilization, based upon the stable food supply of agriculture, made possible the development of cities.

The first hill farmers wandered down into the valley of the two rivers around the year 4000 B.C. Five hundred years later, there was a highly developed culture on the land built around Sumer, the first city in the valley. By 3000 B.C. there were fourteen city-states in the valley of the two rivers. No longer was every man a hunter or a farmer. Human resources had expanded in many directions. In the city-states of Sumeria, specialization came to be typical of human activity. Each man learned one trade and made his own special contribution within that field, as slave, farmer, potter, gemsmith, overseer, engineer, scribe, teacher, astronomer, astrologer, priest, warrior, king, or something else. Nobody learned to do and know everything. That was impossible because the culture had become so very complex. There were experts in every field. Each man mastered his own work and human society grew richer, more varied than ever before.

Specialization brings a great increase in the possible uses of human resources. It makes a great civilization possible. Ever since the days of Sumer, specialization has been a basic characteristic of civilized human culture.

The Egyptians

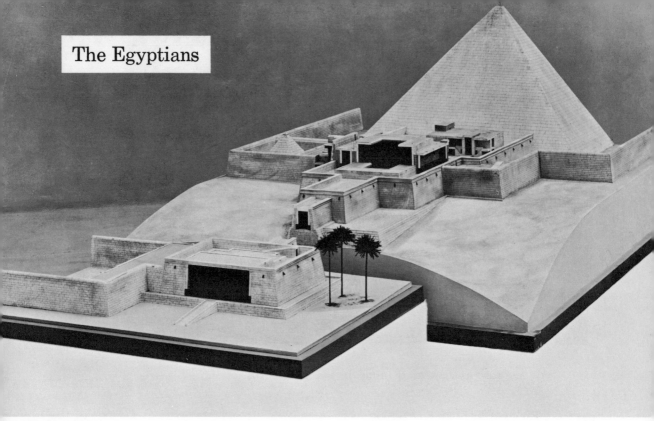

Model of a pyramid.

At the time when the Sumerians were building their civilization, another culture, that of the Egyptians, was thriving along the ten-mile-wide strip of the Nile River valley. The river was the source of water and fertile soil in a large, arid desert region. The Egyptians learned to make use of the rainy season to become skilled farmers, engineers, and artisans. They built irrigation systems to channel the water from the river. They raised cattle, grew crops of grain and flax.

Successful farming along this valuable river valley required close cooperation and a central administration. Local chieftains gave way to a large kingdom. As a result of trade with neighboring peoples, the Egyptians prospered, annexed other areas, and built an empire. Great cities grew with highly advanced cultures.

The Egyptians discovered copper ore in their region and invented copper chisels. They used the river as the highway to transport huge slabs of limestone for the construction of pyramids and temples.

The Egyptians had distinct social classes. The king, the priests, nobles, and scribes formed the aristocracy.

Pictures and pictograph writing describe how sculptures were made.

18

Garments of woven linen and leather, decorated with gold were found intact inside the pyramids.

They were able to read the Egyptian picture language that was inscribed on papyrus rolls and on rocks. They were able to design complicated irrigation and water-management systems. Egyptian priests and scholars studied the moon and the stars. They invented a calendar and a system of mathematics. The aristocrats lived in fine houses of sundried brick and imported wood. They used dishes and other household objects made of gold, silver, copper, and of finely-turned pottery. The ladies of wealth wore

garments of woven cotton decorated with gold and jewels.

Most of the work on the farms, in the quarries, and in the various crafts was done by slaves, as is shown in the statues, monuments, and pyramids that still stand.

Most of what we know about the Egyptian civilization has been handed down through objects, drawings, sculpture, and writings in the tombs and pyramids. Their religion taught that there was a life after death and the objects in the tombs might be useful in the next world.

19

The Persian Empire-Builders

Stairway built in Persian times, gate of King Xerxes at right.

During the days of ancient history, there were many conquerors. First one city gobbled up others; small city-states united into kingdoms; and further expansion led to the building of an empire.

The Assyrians, then the Chaldeans, the Hittites, and the Medes conquered other lands and later fell apart. These great states, in turn, made possible the mingling of cultures and the development of new civilizations. It was the Persians who became the first great empire-builders.

The Persians first rose to power under Cyrus, who lived among the hill people just east of the civilized valley of the Tigris-Euphrates Rivers. He united his people, tribes of poor farmers. He became king of the Persians in 559 B.C. and subdued the Medes to the West, marched into Asia Minor, and destroyed the armies of Lydia. Thirty years and three kings later, the Persians controlled all the lands from Egypt to Greece, on through Babylon to the fringes of India. This was a vast territory. Darius, who completed the conquests, called himself — as he truly was — the King of Kings.

Half a dozen races and over 50 languages were to be found within the empire — hill farmers and nomads, the civilized peoples of Egypt and Babylon, merchant sailors of Syria and Greece, fishermen, wild huntsmen of the high mountains. The Persians organized a system for ruling all of them.

Good government, then as now, required a system of administration and laws, good means of travel and communication, a strong system of defense, and sufficient revenue from taxes to pay for all of these things. Darius was able to achieve unity within his empire by dividing it into twenty-one provinces or satrapies, each under a Persian governor called a satrap. Each satrap had charge of his area and kept in close touch with the king. Garrisons of Persian soldiers were established at key places to keep watch, guard the borders, and crush rebellions.

A good, well-paved Royal Road was built across the empire, some 1,600 miles long, from Sardis in the west to the capital city of Susa. Royal messengers and inspectors could move quickly on this road and royal armies, too, if they were needed. Darius permitted the subject peoples to keep their own customs, laws, and religion so long as they paid their taxes and did not stir up rebellions. Those who rebelled were brutally crushed as chariots thundered in carrying strong, black-bearded Persian soldiers who were quick to hack with their short swords.

In 494 B.C., the Greeks of Ionia rose against their Persian masters. The Persians sent their armies against them; the armies crossed over the Sea of Bosporus and down toward Athens. The Persian might was stopped by the rugged terrain and the fierce resistance of the Greeks. Additional armies were sent in, but the Persians could never conquer Greece. And so, after many campaigns, they pulled back to Asia Minor. They remained the mighty neighbors of the Greeks, but not their overlords.

Metropolitan Museum of Art

Valiant Greek soldier fighting against the Persians, inscribed on a vase.

Greek Civilization

Model of Delphi, showing Temple of Apollo.

The Greeks began as farmers and shepherds eking out an existence on poor soil in a rocky, mountainous region; yet they managed to become one of the greatest civilizations of all times. They lived around the Aegean Sea and on all the islands of that sea, down to the large island of Crete. When they conquered Crete, they acquired a highly civilized culture. From the Cretans and from all the many peoples that they met as their empire grew, the Greeks learned.

The Greek Empire extended throughout southern Italy and to Sicily, which became part of greater Greece. The Greeks then moved on to the southern coasts of the Black Sea and places along the northern shores. They had colonies in North Africa, Spain, and southern France. The Greeks became a seafaring people, having learned navigation and commerce from their subjects. They sailed throughout and far beyond their far-flung empire. They met the peoples of Egypt, Persia, and Babylon. They saw the Scythian horsemen of the northern steppes; black Nubians of Africa; pale, painted and tattooed men from Britain;

blond traders in amber from the Baltic; lordly Etruscans; hard-bargaining Phoenicians. The Greeks met civilization and savagery in many forms. They learned from all the cultures, and as we shall see, they later served as an inspiration to the people who conquered them.

Remains of the Parthenon.

Since the Greeks no longer depended upon farming on poor soil, they developed commerce. They had trading centers in all their colonies and eventually there was a large prosperous middle class. From the civilized peoples of Egypt and Persia the Greeks learned shipbuilding, mathematics, astronomy, iron working, brass founding, and surveying. They became travelers, warriors, craftsmen and merchants. They achieved greatness in their painting, architecture, and sculpture. The Greeks also became writers. They wrote in an alphabet system based on that of the Sumerians and other early people.

The Greeks wrote about the strange lands and peoples of the uncivilized world. They wrote down the legends of their own people and the true stories of warfare and heroes. They wrote of their gods, kings, and the plain people. Greek writers wrote beautiful poetry and drama.

Like other ancient peoples, the Greeks worshipped gods of nature but they separated religion from government and began to seek solutions to problems outside of ritual, superstition, and the supernatural. Gradually, this release of the human mind led to new political patterns and a form of democracy. Under their system of government, each citizen enjoyed the privileges as well as the responsibilities of citizenship. Rights were assigned to slaves as well as to citizens.

Greek culture spread throughout the Mediterranean world and became the basis for modern Western civilization.

New York Stock Exchange

Greek style architecture may be seen throughout the world. N.Y. Stock Exchange Building.

Greek Philosophy And Science

Athens was the intellectual capital of the Greek world. It was a small city but it had great influence. In Athens lived philosophers, writers, and artists who met with one another, exchanged ideas, and had the freedom to express what they believed.

The Greeks believed that the world was an orderly universe governed by laws which man could understand. They became philosophers. They were the first to ask why things work as they do. They wanted to understand the world as well as live in it — and they expected to understand in rational terms. They spent a lot of time talking, arguing, discussing, and asking questions. To the Greeks, this abstract thinking was known as *philosophy,* meaning love of wisdom. The philosophers would analyze the conditions, and especially the ideals, of human behavior. The scholars studied nature and nature's laws. The "natural philosophy" of the Greeks came to be known as *science,* derived from the Roman word that means to know.

Abstract thought, science, and philosophy are great achievements of the human mind. Without them the modern world, as we know it, could never have come into existence. Many of the Greek philosophers and scientists are still known and admired. Pythagoras, who lived at the end of the 6th century B.C. in southern Italy, formulated the laws of musical harmony. He founded a mysterious brotherhood dedicated to discovering the mathematical laws of the universe. Plato, an aristocrat who lived in the middle of the 4th century B.C., was a follower of Pythagoras and of the great philosopher, Socrates. Plato's writings are still the foundations of philosophical thought.

The most famous of all Greek thinkers was Aristotle, a student of Plato. Aristotle, son of a physician from Macedon, was tutor to the son of King Philip, young Alexander — later to become Alexander the Great. Aristotle established a school in Athens and spent the rest of his life teaching, arguing, thinking, and writing. His works filled some 140 volumes and dealt with logic, ethics, metaphysics, political science, literary criticism, and more. Aristotle made keen observations of the natural world around him and wrote down what he saw. For this reason, he is known as the world's first scientist. For many centuries, Aristotle's observations were fundamental to the study of physics, mechanics, meteorology, optics, botany, zoology, astronomy, and cosmology. Can you see why Aristotle merits his great fame?

There were many other great intellectuals among the Greeks including scientists, historians, mathematicians, ethnographers, grammarians, librarians, and philologists. Euclid's textbook in geometry was used until the twentieth century; Hero and Archimedes wrote basic works in physics; Aristarchus recorded his ideas of astronomy; Galen and Hippocrates wrote about medicine; Pto-

Socrates, a great teacher and philosopher, was ordered to drink poison because he was thought to be influencing young minds to raise questions. The scene was painted by Jacques Louis David, noted French artist.

lemy studied astronomy and geography. These are just a few of many Greek scholars and philosophers.

Although Greek thinkers aimed to understand the world, not control it, the Greeks came to do that as well. In the course of ten short years, ending in 324 B.C., Alexander of Macedon led his armies to conquer the whole of the Persian Empire. Through conquest the Greeks spread their culture to the civilized world. Greek cities were established in Persia, Asia, and Egypt. Alexandria, a Greek city near the mouth of the Nile, was founded and named by Alexander. It was to become a new center of science and philosophy inspiring such Greek thinkers as Hero, Archimedes, Aristarchus, and Ptolemy.

And so the newer Greek civilization spread abstract thought, philosophy, and science among the ancient civilizations of Egypt, Babylon, and India.

Travelers Ins.

The Roman Forum, scene of public discussions.

The successors to the Greek Empire were the Romans — the military conquerors of Greece, but in reality the Greeks were the cultural conquerors. The Romans passed down the Greek civilization to the generations that followed.

The Romans were originally an obscure tribe of farmers who lived on the plains of Latium in central Italy under the dominion of foreign Etruscan kings. They rose in arms during the sixth century B.C. and drove out their foreign masters. Then they went on to subdue all the other small tribes of Latium. From there the Romans turned and conquered the Etruscans to the north, and the Greek cities of southern Italy. By the beginning of the third century, their capital, Rome, was a great city, the master of all Italy.

The Romans went on to conquer much of the known world: Sicily, North Africa, Sardinia and Spain, France, Germany west of the Rhine River, Greece, Romania and Bulgaria, Egypt and all the lands west of Babylon. During the first century B. C., Julius Caesar added distant Britain to the empire of Rome.

The Roman Empire was centered around the Mediterranean Sea. It took in all the civilized world west of Persia, many peoples and many tribes, speaking many tongues and dialects. In the western half, from Spain and Britain to Italy, most people spoke Latin, the language of Rome, though many farmers and tribesmen of the forest or desert spoke local dialects and tongues. In the eastern half, Greek continued to be the language of the upper classes, of government officials, merchants and all educated people, as it had been since the days of Alexander.

The Romans admired all aspects of Greek culture. They regarded Greek schools as the best in the world, and Greek writings in literature, philosophy, science, mathematics, and the arts as unexcelled by any other. Aristocrats of Rome and the Empire were sending their sons to Greek schools in Athens or Alexandria. In time any well-educated Roman Senator could deliver long orations in Greek; one Emperor of Rome even kept his personal diary in Greek. Although Roman civilization and Latin writings also flourished, the greatest language of civilization remained Greek.

Like the Persians, the Romans tied their far-flung domain together by constructing good roads. They launched ships upon the seas, kept armies to guard the frontiers, built fortresses and garrisons and encouraged the economic as well as cultural development of their subjects. The Romans spread public works throughout the lands under their control. They built arched stone bridges over rivers and streams, aqueducts of durable concrete, and many fine public buildings and homes. The remains of Roman engineering and architecture can still be seen in modern France, Britain, Greece, Egypt, and other lands.

The Romans brought a new political ideal to the world — the rule of law. Roman law prevailed throughout the empire, not a separate law for every tribe and people. Justice was open to all men, not just a few. Roman laws and court decisions were written down for all to understand. Their system of law has influenced the laws under which Americans, British, French, and many other modern people live. It stressed equality before the law, the principle that a man was innocent until proven guilty, that an accused man must have the right to face his accusers, and more.

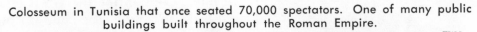

Colosseum in Tunisia that once seated 70,000 spectators. One of many public buildings built throughout the Roman Empire.

TWA

The Fall Of Rome

Rome also became the refuge and center of Christianity. After years of prosperity and world power, the ruling class became indifferent to the poverty of the masses of people. A new r e l i g i o n was being spread through the empire by the followers of Jesus, born in Nazareth in the eastern part of the Roman Empire and crucified three hundred years earlier. The Christians preached a belief in one God (monotheism) and not the cult of many gods. Monotheism, first introduced by the Hebrews in ancient Palestine, was the basis of the Christian religion. Christianity appealed to the Roman masses because it taught that suffering in this world would lead to salvation in a future life. It also taught the ideals of equality among men, brotherhood, and humility.

At first, Christians and their sympathizers were arrested and persecuted. Then, in 312 A. D., Emperor Constantine became a Christian, and Christianity became the official religion of Rome.

Latin language was kept alive by religious manuscripts.

But then at last, in the fourth century, after hundreds of years of power and dominion, the great Roman Empire began to crack and fall apart. Since it was too big to rule from one center, Constantine the Great established two capital cities, one at Rome and the other at Constantinople. He moved his own court to the new city and appointed an assistant emperor to live in Rome. From that time on the two halves of the empire, one Greek, the other Latin, began to drift apart.

In the western part, civil wars broke out. The frontiers were left unguarded. Barbarian giants rode in from the north, mounted on swift horses, striking down the small foot soldiers of Rome. These barbarians seized whatever they wanted, carved the great empire into lands and regions of their own, and called them-

Emperor Constantine (272-337 A.D.) first Christian Roman emperor.

selves kings. The emperors of the East were powerless to strike back. So the western empire disappeared leaving only a confusion of barbarian kingdoms and the widespread skeleton of the Christian church.

The years from the 4th or 5th century to the 13th century A. D. saw a serious setback to civilization in western Europe. Swords rang out in the forests; superstition, fear, and ignorance flourished; populations declined, and civilization based on the development of the human mind was repressed. The Greek language was lost and the Latin language nearly disappeared; instead, barbarian tongues were heard throughout the continent.

St. Peter's Basilica, Vatican City. Site on which public spectacles were made of Christian persecution.

Only the church survived, trying to carry on its traditions, using the Latin language as its means of communication and the city of Rome as its center. The only light in the "dark ages" that f o l l o w e d came t h r o u g h the Christian churches, which gave refuge to people from a troubled, violent world.

Romans in battle on the plains of Chalon, France.

29

World Cultures During The Early Middle Ages

Western civilization was crumbling from neglect, disorder, and continual warfare during the period between the 5th and 13th centuries A.D. People s e e k i n g protection against invaders gathered together under local leaders, each of whom would build a fortress on a high point. There was a return to small kingdoms u n d e r petty kings and lords. This gave rise to feudalism by which, for 1,000 years, people were ruled with an iron hand by the individual or family in power at a particular time.

The only influence that kept the European civilization from total destruction was the universal acceptance of the Christian religion under the leadership of a single Pope in Rome. Some very religious individuals, known as monks, withdrew from the trials and problems of the political world and dedicated themselves to working in behalf of the church. They were the ones who spent long hours copying the Bible, keeping records, and preserving some of the wisdom inherited from R o m e and Greece.

The social organization of a typical feudal manor during early Middle Ages. Upper picture: clergy, lord of the manor, his lay counselors, and warriors. Lower left. bourgeoisie and artisans, tradesmen, artists. Lower right: serfs.

Plains Indians of North America. Painting
by A.A. Jansson.

Detail of a wall of the Mexican Pyramid
of the Sun.

During these same centuries, man's
genius was at work in other parts of
the world. Great civilizations were
developing in China, India, and
among the Mayan and Inca Indians
of the Western Hemisphere. In the
area around Constantinople, once the
eastern capital of the Roman Empire,
many institutions of Roman law and
justice were continued under the
Byzantine culture.

Bronze figure,
India.

Woodcut of a Japanese procession.

Japanese and Chinese painting reflect the beauty of the landscape and
the continuity of movement. The paintings are often on silk or rice paper,
in the form of hangings. The viewer unrolls the painting, bit by bit, to
glimpse an unfolding scene. Chinese art forms also reflect the influence of
invading armies from the Fertile Crescent.

The Renaissance

TWA

Renaissance cathedral, Chartres, France.

During the period 1400 to 1500, there was a renewed interest in culture and knowledge throughout the western world. This was seen in the three strands of the Renaissance, the Reformation, and the Scientific Revolution.

The Renaissance is the period of history that revived an interest in scholarship and the arts.

In Italy, scholars became interested in old Greek and Latin manuscripts. They translated the writings of Pythagoras, Homer, Plato, Aristotle,

Herodotus, St. Paul, Galen, Ptolemy, St. Basil and hundreds of other classical writers. To these they added newly discovered works of Roman writers. These Greek and Roman works, so long hidden and forgotten, now reappeared and swelled the great stream of books, which were being produced on the newly-invented printing presses.

The rediscovery of Greek was most important. It brought forth an unimagined wisdom which had been unknown in the western lands since the fall of the Roman Empire, but which in many areas went far beyond anything the Romans or the Middle Ages had ever produced. Translations from the Greek played such an important part in reviving artistic, scientific, and analytical studies that the Italians began to speak of their age as a Renaissance or "rebirth" of ancient Greece.

Artists like Michelangelo, Raphael, Titian, Leonardo da Vinci, and Giorgione; architects like Alberti and Palladio; philosophers like Ficino, Pico della Mirandola, and other members of the Platonic Academy, all of these and many others were inspired by the ideals of ancient Greece.

From Italy, the great intellectual explosion of the Renaissance spread to all of western Europe by means of printed books, teachers, writers, artists, and travelers.

In the last half of the fifteenth century, a great expansion of European civilization brought the Middle Ages to a rapid end. This expansion was like an explosion in its force. First it changed the very nature of civiliza-

in der welt lyt wan als verr jerusalem von mittozen landen lyt/also verr lyt
es ouch von jndien das ober land heit wañ es heist Ozient das ist der sunnen
pffgang/vnd das jerusalem mitten in derse/oz bewiset da mit weñ man pff
den mittentag ein gleffi pffrich
tet zů jerusalem so git sie keinen
schattë pff die sitte/als sie tůt in
disen landë oz ist so tag vñ nacht
glich lang sind. vnd ouch zů jeru
salem ist gar ein tůffi pfůtz wer
dar in steiger in der zitt des jars/
so tag vñ nacht gleich seint oz die
sonn glich ob im ist/vnnd da by
merckt man das jerusalem mit
ten in der welt sy/vnnd des git
ouch kúnig david gezúgnús/da
er sprich in dem psalter·Et ope
ratus est in medio terre·Das ist
zů tůsch Gott het vnser heil ge·

Page from a book of travels printed in German in Strassburg, 1483.

tion within Europe, then it thrust outwards and marked the beginning of the modern world.

Technology gave this cultural explosion much of its power in the form of the printing press, invented around the year 1450 by Johannes Gutenberg of Mainz, Germany.

Gutenberg invented the system of using movable type. Before his time, each page of copy was carved on a w o o d e n block, and then passed through a press resembling a wine press. The new method enabled the printer to shape and cast each letter or numeral in a mold. There were different sizes and designs of type that could be interchanged. Individual l e t t e r s were assembled to form words, sentences, and paragraphs. The carved illustrations were then added and the page was ready for the press. After the run was completed, the letters were taken out, sorted, and filed to be used over again.

Soon after the new m e t h o d of printing appeared, o t h e r printers adopted it. The areas between northern Italy and the Netherlands became a center of printing and publishing. Printing spread throughout western Europe from Poland to England, from Sweden to Sicily. Even in faraway Spain, the university town of Salamanca had 52 printing presses and 84 booksellers by the year 1500.

So great was the interest in books that, in the city of Venice alone, some two million books were printed between 1450 and 1500. More than that, books appeared on all subjects in which people were interested, and in the local languages. The printing press helped to spread knowledge about new movements in religion, science, and the arts.

The Reformation And Scientific Revolution

In northern Europe, books, printing, and the Renaissance gave birth to two further explosions of ideas — the Reformation and the Scientific Revolution.

Erasmus of Rotterdam studied in Italian universities and then went to live in England. He was a Renaissance man and studied the ancient gospels and epistles of the New Testament, since they had been written in Greek during the days of the Roman Empire. He compared many old manuscripts, wrote many notes, and finally, after long years of labor, he prepared a very accurate edition of the whole New Testament in Greek. It was printed, complete with footnotes, in a Latin translation and sold throughout Europe.

Far off in Germany, a monk named Martin Luther bought the book, read it and was strengthened in his conviction that true Christian religion must be based solely on the writings of the Bible. Thus he attacked many of the practices and beliefs of the Catholic Church, which at that time was the only church in western Europe. The result was a great religious explosion which shattered the unity of Christendom, established many churches and a rich variety of religious thought, practice and belief, led to a new individualism and finally to the principle of tolerance for the differing beliefs of others.

During Luther's lifetime, another churchman, Nicholas Copernicus of Poland, wrote a book to prove that

Copernicus, a Polish monk who dared to challenge the view that the earth was the center of the universe.

Travelers Ins.

the sun, not the earth, was at the center of the universe. He had studied at Italian universities and had become familiar with the writings of the ancient Greek philosopher, Aristarchus, who had also said that the earth went around the sun. Copernicus tried to revive this ancient theory of Aristarchus, which opposed the accepted belief of Aristotle that the earth was the center of the universe. Copernicus touched off a long scholarly debate on astronomy. Many hundreds of books and pamphlets were written on this and other scientific subjects about which the ancient Greeks had other opinions.

Galileo demonstrating his improved telescope, Genoa, 1609.

The year 1500 is the turning point of history. In that year, Michelangelo, Martin Luther, Erasmus, and Copernicus were all alive. Since that year, the new civilization of Science and Technology was born in the expansion of Europe.

The Scientific Revolution introduced the scientific method, by which ideas are tested again and again under laboratory conditions. Tycho Brahe (1546-1601), a Danish astronomer, and Galileo (1564-1642), an Italian scientist, made important discoveries during this time. The unending curiosity of people in all lands during all periods of history was given great impetus by the development of the scientific method and the invention of improved instruments.

35

Exploration And Discovery

Land, the island of San Salvadaor, is finally sighted by Columbus and his crew.

Travelers Ins.

Christopher Columbus was also living in the year 1500. Eight years before, he had sailed westward from S p a i n and discovered the New World. Half a century before Columbus, Portuguese explorers had sailed southward along the coast of West Africa, past deserts, past jungles, past the lands of brown and black-skinned peoples, past capes and had come at last to India.

The knowledge of shipbuilding made it possible for them to sail around the world. They had large full-hulled ships with many masts and m a n y sails carrying rich cargoes. They had good maps, compasses, astrolabes, and an accumulated science of high-seas navigation. Equipped with new forms of weapons and armor, they could c o n q u e r nearly everywhere they sailed.

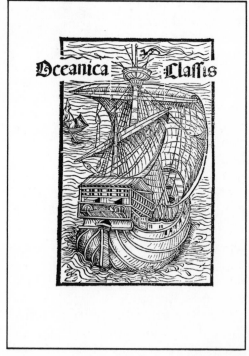

N. Y. Public Library

Illustration from **Letter to Sanchez** by Christopher Columbus, published in 1493.

36

In the decades after Columbus, European ships sailed everywhere. This was the era of discovery and exploration. From all parts of the globe, the explorers and traders brought back valuable products, many of them quite unknown — tobacco, corn, cocoa, and potatoes from America; gold and silver from Mexico and Peru; clove, cinnamon, pepper, and tea f r o m the Orient; calico, muslin, madras, and serge from India; silk and jade from China; diamonds, ivory, and slaves from Africa.

By the early sixteenth century, the European economy had become the first world-wide economy in the history of mankind.

Nations competed with one another for new lands to control. By the beginning of the seventeenth century, small colonies of Europeans could be found in many distant places. There were Spaniards in Florida, the Carribean, Mexico, Panama,

South America, and the Philippines. There were Portuguese merchants and settlers in Japan, Macao, Goa, Africa, and Brazil. There were Dutch settlements in Asia and Africa. There were English, Swedish, Dutch, and French colonies in North America.

Before the end of the eighteenth century, the Europeans in North America had founded a new nation, having broken their political ties with Europe by a revolution, and having established the United States of America.

This, then, has been a brief but impressive review of man's rise over thousands of years from hunter to empire builder, scientist, and humanitarian. It has been a story of constructive achievements as well as wanton destruction and c r u e l t y among peoples. Man changes, he progresses, but he remains man for better or worse. Old problems are solved, but new ones constantly arise.

Pioneers build settlements in the New World more than 200 years after discovery.

CHAPTER 2

MAN AND HIS WORK

Astronaut Edward White stepped out of his spacecraft in June 1965 and "walked" about the planet earth. In doing so he fulfilled the dreams of a thousand years and more. He was like Icarus of Greek mythology, who dared to fly close to the sun, except that the wings of Icarus melted and he plunged to his death, while Edward White came safely back to earth. He was like the winged man sketched in Leonardo da Vinci's notebook some five hundred years ago. He was also like Superman, flying through space in a red cape.

Many men have had such dreams. Any man with imagination can dream and see himself hurtling through space, leaping over mountains, encircling the world. But dreams and fantasies are one thing and facts another. Edward White's walk was a fact. It took work as well as imagination. Many men worked for many years, all of them specialists — astrophysicists, mathematicians, rocket engineers, astronomers, geometers, industrialists, computer analysts, test pilots, generals, electricians, riveters, politicians, doctors, dieticians, even taxpayers had a share along with many others. It took cooperation and it took many years of careful work, study, experimentation, planning. No one man could do it. It took hundreds of men working together, each an expert in his own area. It took the widespread resources of a great nation and help from abroad besides.

Even at that, only a small part of America's productivity was drawn upon to put Edward White into space. This land is great in dreams and great in resources. Its people have used these resources to make dreams into reality.

The story of man's physical and mental labors to achieve our modern scientific and technological excellence is told through history. It is the story of inventions riding piggyback on other inventions; of a vast and eager work force set free in a new land; of a complex system of commerce and industry strengthened by abundant resources, a continual supply of labor and growing capital for investment.

Americans once worked together to civilize the wilderness. They now work together to provide a decent standard of living for more and more people. Who knows what future Americans can accomplish with even greater resourcefulness?

Pan Am Building

Bureau of Reclamation, Dept. of Interior

Improving Man's Tools

In the hundreds of centuries from Paleolithic times through the civilizations of antiquity, all of man's work was performed by human muscle power. After man learned to use animals for hauling heavy loads and as a source of power for plows, mills and vehicles, his efficiency improved. Clever minds devised simple tools and elaborate mechanical devices — yet, most work depended upon vast numbers of workers.

The pyramids of Egypt were built with human labor, not by the power of oxen or elephants. The great marble temples of Greece and the highways and aqueducts of the Romans were built with slave labor. Where there are large numbers of people to do the work and where governments have limited funds with which to carry out great engineering projects, human labor is still used in the 20th century as in the civilizations of old.

As the nations of the world began to rebuild their cities and highways in the Middle Ages, they had to improve their ways of working to replace the outlawed institutions of slavery and serfdom. Better technology was needed. Technology is the production and use of tools. It has been part of human culture since the days of the earliest people. Today's technology consists of machines, mechanical devices, computers, jet planes, and all the tools of modern living.

Since civilizations are always dependent upon a source of food, one of the greatest inventions might be listed as the Saxon plow, invented early in the Middle Ages somewhere north of the Roman Empire. It was a large-wheeled plow, pulled by many horses or oxen. It could turn the thick, wet soils of northwestern Europe, as well as the bogs and forests of the North into productive farmlands. The plow made possible the expansion of population in northwestern Europe and helped to change the people from wandering barbarians to settled farmers. Even the knights began to settle down and build castles.

Other important inventions used the wheel to harness wind and water power. Wheels had been used for animal-drawn chariots and carts as well as to fashion clay into fine vases. But the wheel and axle as a mechanical device to control the flow of power began with the waterwheel. The weight of the water would push the wheel, making it turn. This, then, would cause a machine to move. In the Netherlands, since the 12th century, machines were attached to a wind-wheel because wind was more plentiful than water.

At first the energy from the moving water and wind was used to grind grain into flour. By the end of the Middle Ages, it was used for spinning and weaving cloth, beating rags into pulp for paper, sawing logs, grinding tools, and for many other machines.

Later, when James Watt invented an engine powered by steam, it began a whole new way of working and living and caused an Industrial Revolution.

In Mysore, India, modern machines aided by 40,000 laborers build a power plant and dam to improve living standards for millions of people. Compare with Egyptian pyramid builders who toiled to produce monuments for their rulers.

Boston Museum of Science

Iron and Steel Institute

Netherlands Inf. Service

A.I.D., Dept of State

The Industrial Revolution

An early British steam engine, built in 1800.

The Industrial Revolution began in England and western Europe in the mid-1700's and spread to the New World. It changed people's ways of working, but it also changed their ways of living more rapidly than any other development previously known. Before the mechanization of industry, most people lived on the land or in cities and produced what they needed with simple tools and implements at home. People had very little money, no education, and the standard of living was low.

The developments in science and knowledge and the growth of markets during the 17th and 18th centuries created a condition that paved the way for human inventiveness and imagination. When inventors and dreamers were aided by people with capital, a whole new method of pro-

duction could be used. Workers came to new factories to operate machines and to produce large quantities of textiles, clothing, household goods, farm machinery, and the like. Most workers had to give up home crafts and go to work in factories to earn a living. City populations grew rapidly, as did trade and wealth.

The factory system spread to the United States. Samuel Slater, a worker in an English textile mill, became familiar with the system of producing cloth by large machines. He learned every process of operating a textile factory and wrote to a wealthy Quaker merchant in Rhode Island: "Both of us can grow rich through my knowledge. I can build from memory the machinery needed for a cotton factory." The American merchant agreed and they entered into a partnership. A year later their textile factory in Pawtucket, Rhode Island was in active production. The machines drew power from a waterfall. In the years that followed, many other factories were built and new towns sprang up beside the rivers and waterfalls of New England.

Child labor was common in the early factories.

The Industrial Revolution influenced the ways of working on plantations in the South. To pick and clean cotton and separate the boll from the seed required long, tedious work by many people — in this case, slave laborers. Eli Whitney invented a machine that improved the operation. Where it once took a skilled worker a whole day to clean four pounds of cotton, the cotton gin increased his output to 50 pounds a day. Between better and cheaper methods of growing cotton and similar improvements in weaving it into yarn, mass production was on its way.

Since necessity is the mother of invention, the increased demand for machine goods called for better power than that of water or wind. After some attempts by a few inventors, James Watt produced a steam engine in 1800 that was very efficient. Coal was needed to produce the steam and the iron for the machines; therefore, the Industrial Revolution had its influence on the mining industries, too.

What about the people who performed the work? At first the home craftsmen feared the machines. They saw their handmade products replaced by goods that could be turned out faster and cheaper — sometimes better. Some workers rioted, broke into factories and smashed the machines. Others quietly closed their home workshops and took jobs in factories. They looked forward to steady wages and a better life.

Unfortunately, the workers found new problems facing them. Working hours were long and pay was small. Women and children had to join the men to help eke out an adequate family wage. Homes in cities and towns were crowded together in narrow streets. Conditions in factories were unsanitary and unsafe.

A New World: A New Way Of Life

George Washington Bicentennial Commission

George Washington and his Cabinet: Secretary of War, Henry Knox; Secretary of The Treasury, Alexander Hamilton; Secretary of State, Thomas Jefferson; Attorney General, Edmund Randolph.

See the American colonies around the time of George Washington's inauguration. Here was western civilization transplanted to the wilderness of a vast new land. Here were families from many cultures building a new life for themselves and a revolutionary idea in self-government. The form of government which was established during Washington's administration proclaimed: "We, the people of the United States, do ordain and establish this Constitution for the United States of America." It specifically stated that all men are by nature equally free and independent. The new government was unlike any that had been known in Europe. It was based on a philosophy that the government existed only with the consent of the governed. The young nation stirred the imagination of statesmen, explorers, farmers, workers, adventurers. People came from all parts of the western world, even from Asia.

Northern states were settled mainly by families from England and France. The soil was rocky and the climate harsh. Help from all members of the family was needed to eke out an existence from the land. As a result, some of the sons and daughters of farmers moved to towns and growing cities. There they swelled the ranks of laborers, tradesmen, craftsmen, blacksmiths, and others. Some remained in the labor force; others became bankers, rich merchants, ministers, or teachers.

Fishermen, sailors, merchants, and shipwrights lived in the coastal towns. Clipper ships sailed from the ports of New England, laden with furs, fish, tar, pitch, and lumber. They sailed to the seaports of England and Europe, and also to Africa, the Caribbean Sea, and to far-off China. After many months they returned with tools, wagons, cloth, books, spices, tea, chocolate, whale bone and oil, even silks, fine china, furniture, and costly silver.

Yankee clipper ships.   Paramount Pictures

Prairie schooners moving westward.   20th Century-Fox

The colonists produced grain, timber, tobacco, fine horses, whiskey and many kinds of seafood for export. They provided a profitable market for manufactured items produced in England and other European nations. The middle colonies, like those of New England, were settled by people from northern Europe. Most important, however, was the mixture of creeds and races that settled and lived together. There were Catholics, Lutherans, Quakers, Jews, Pennsylvania Dutch, and a wide range of Protestants.

Settlers to the South included aristocrats from England and France. They found a mild climate and rich soils that were suitable for agriculture — crops that needed long, moderate growing seasons such as rice, tobacco, indigo, cotton. Southern ports sent out huge cargoes of these products and received gold, silver, and luxuries from distant lands. These ports also received slaves.

The slave trade was not limited to southern plantation owners. Newport, Rhode Island was a busy port of entry for the slaves. From there they were sent to southern ports in exchange for sugar, tobacco and other products, which were sent to the West Indies where sugar was changed to rum — and rum shipped to the African slave traders. The extent of slave trading can be seen from the following figures. In 1708 there were 12,000 Negroes in Virginia; in 1715 there were 23,000; in 1743, 42,000, and by 1782 (almost at the time of Washington's inauguration) there were 260,000 in that single state.

Colonial stage coach.   Warner Bros.

New Methods, New Jobs

Globe

Vast numbers of the immigrants arrived in America as unskilled workers. Many of them found work in the new factories. Some became garment or textile workers, tailors and hatters, shoemakers and glovemakers; others sweated in steel mills, mines, shipyards, glass factories, potteries, and brickyards; and some worked in factories that made machines for other factories.

Building railroad and telegraph lines across the land, 1869.

Southern Pacific

Meanwhile, mechanization was bringing the Industrial Revolution to the agricultural countryside as well. Factory-made farm machinery like McCormick's reaper, invented in 1834, and new scientific farming methods brought greater agricultural yields with less manpower. Along with mechanization came specialization. Huge cattle ranches spread over the plains states from Texas to North Dakota. In the Far West, orchards and vineyards were planted on irrigated fields. Food processing factories were built in the farming regions — creameries, dairies and cheese factories, stockyards, canning plants, breweries, mills, and others. The farm laborers, no longer needed on the land, worked in these industries or moved to the cities to swell the ranks of urban workers.

At the same time, industrial growth brought new systems of transportation, communication, and business organization. A network of roads, canals and railroads spread across the whole nation, while steamships plied the rivers, coastlines and the Great Lakes. Raw materials could now be brought to factories

McCormick's reaper.   Keystone View Co.

Railroads and telegraph help build new industry, new towns, new jobs, Beaumont, Texas during an oil boom, 1901.

and finished merchandise could then be hauled back to cities and to seaports for shipment abroad.

New networks of communication were built. The first regular mail system used couriers and pony express, then the mails moved by rail and steam packet. New inventions, the telegraph, telephone, transoceanic cable and, at last, wireless telegraphy, gave unprecedented speed and convenience to communication. This bound together the whole vast continent of North America. The transoceanic cable put America in instant contact with Europe, still the center of Western civilization.

Expanding business organizations also went mechanical. They were quick to adopt such efficient new devices as the typewriter, telegraph, and adding machine. This mechanization of office procedures resulted in a whole new class of "white collar" workers — secretaries, clerks, accountants, and the like.

There were many kinds of workers in an increasingly specialized society. There were those who labored on farms and in stores and food factories. There were "white collar" workers of offices and "blue collar" workers of the shops and factories. There were increasing numbers of professional people, doctors, dentists, teachers, lawyers, architects, and professors. Expanding government responsibilities led to a growing class of civil service workers and military personnel. The prospering nation needed many kinds of talents in its people.

Machines for the Great Plains.

During the early 1800's there was a great push westward across the mountains into the great unknown North American continent. Here were valleys waiting for a plow. As the frontier moved westward, there was more and more room for farmers. Though industry was growing, nine out of ten Americans were still farmers.

America needed men. She needed farmers to work the wide prairies of the Midwest. She needed boatmen to sail her rivers and seacoasts, laborers to build the railroads across this vast land, lumberjacks, fishermen, factory workers, craftsmen, machinists and miners; the labor of men, women and children — and so they came.

Looking forward to a new life.

Immigrants streamed in from all the world. Some built the railroads that were needed. Teams of Irish workers began from the east, Chinese from the west and they met at last, after thousands of miles and millions of ties, in Utah.

Many Chinese colonies were founded in the western states. Irish immigrants came in such numbers that they seemed to settle everywhere throughout America.

Farmers from Germany, Norway, Scotland and Sweden came to the New World, drove their covered wagons overland, put their plows to the midwestern plains and challenged the bitter winters to grow grain for the nation. Norwegians came as lumberjacks to the northwestern forests where they worked alongside crews of French Canadians. Polish immigrants became farmers or city workers. Czechs, Hungarians and Yugoslavs came to work in the mines of Pennsylvania and Minnesota. Welsh and Swedish laborers, who had been miners in their native land, became farmers, machinists, and white-collar workers in America. Some Italians settled in California as fishermen and keepers of vineyards, but most of them settled in the eastern and midwestern cities together with Russian, German, Polish, Irish, English, Scandinavian and Spanish immigrants — all to become Americans.

New England fishermen.

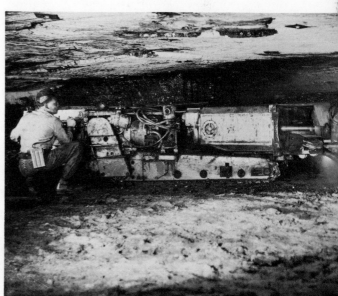

Miners to dig the coal.

Industrial Growth

Mass production then . . . .   Ford Motor

Mass production today . . .   Ford Motor

Industries and businesses expanded in size and number. Machines became larger and more complicated. Some equipment was so expensive that no single individual could afford to buy it. No individual, for example, could afford to pay for a whole railroad — right-of-way, tracks, ties, stations in every town, engines, cars, cabooses, as well as a payroll of thousands of employees.

So businessmen and others with money to invest pooled their money in regular portions, called shares, and formed business organizations known as corporations. These men, known as capitalists, provided the money or capital for a business and lived on the profits earned by their investments. Under this system, factories and industries could expand enormously using the capital to pay for labor and equipment. Ever more costly and complex equipment, larger amounts of raw material converted into greater numbers and varieties of products, wider and wider markets, more and more consumers — these were the things associated with 19th century American capitalism.

Early in our century, Henry Ford introduced the system of mass production to the manufacture of automobiles. He got the idea of the assembly line. Machine-made parts could flow on a moving belt past workers, each one trained to repeat one quick, simple operation. At the end, finished cars would roll off with great speed, regularity, and economy of labor. This method reduced the price of cars and increased demand. Ford also realized that if he paid each man a fair wage, his employees would be able to buy more goods of all kinds, including cars. Since his time, the assembly line and mass production have been applied to many industries. The result has been an enormous increase in productivity

Machines that keep pace with the demand.   Allied Chemical

and this, in turn, has created more goods at lower cost.

All industries are interdependent today, requiring the products of other industries. Growth in one area is reflected by changes in other areas of the economy. Research has become an important part of industrial and governmental growth. The government itself is becoming more closely integrated into the general economy with every passing day. Advertising — using magazines, newspapers, radio, and television, plays a vital role in the growth of industries and in the publicizing of new and changing ones.

Even within this framework of vast farms and immense businesses, however, there is still a need for small, individual enterprises. The skills and services of small shopkeepers, handworkers and repairmen, independent service agencies, and their trained employees are essential to the smooth functioning of daily life in an industrialized society. Specialists of many kinds in industry, civil and military service, and the professions, continue to play an important part in the growing society of Industrial America.

A Local auto repair mechanic. Standard Oil (NJ)

Auto repair and the small shopkeeper are important in each community. Standard Oil (NJ)

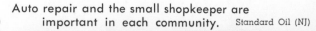

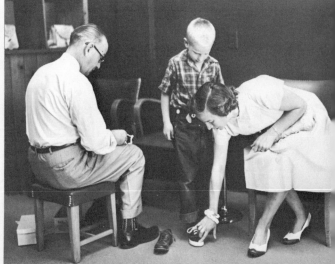

Mass Production And A Higher Standard Of Living

The boom of business expansion in the new factories contributed to the growth of the nation, but by the middle of the 19th century population growth was running far ahead of the available jobs. Immigrants kept streaming into the land in huge numbers. Many of them were illiterate in their own language and unable to speak the English language. There were not enough jobs for all, so they competed for the few jobs that did exist. This competition drove wages down, but any job was better than nothing even at very low wages.

Industrial workers throughout the nation joined together in unions through which they could demand better working conditions, more pay, and other benefits. Employers were reluctant to meet the demands because they believed that low wages were necessary to keep production costs down and profits high. Today, American workers have improved their conditions by contracts between unions and management, by legislation, and by a revised policy of employers toward the needs of workers. Gradually the battle to increase workers' purchasing power has brought gains to industry and the country as well.

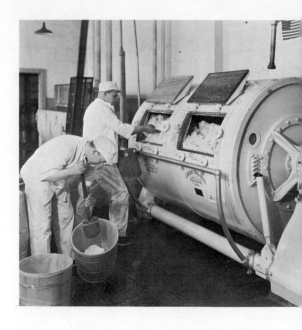

American industrialization has spread to every corner of the country. Through the rise of industry, small farms grew to mighty agricultural empires, capable of feeding the millions of people in crowded cities. Agricultural industries in outlying places gave work to those laborers who were no longer needed in the fields and thus they became the centers of new cities and towns in every state. Giant corporations, aided by capital, science, invention and the work of many hands, extended their operations to meet competition. Branch factories, sales agencies, service organizations, and other affiliates of large industries gave employment throughout the country. Purchasing power grew as workers became the consumers of the things they helped produce and this in turn brought even further industrial expansion.

ILGWU

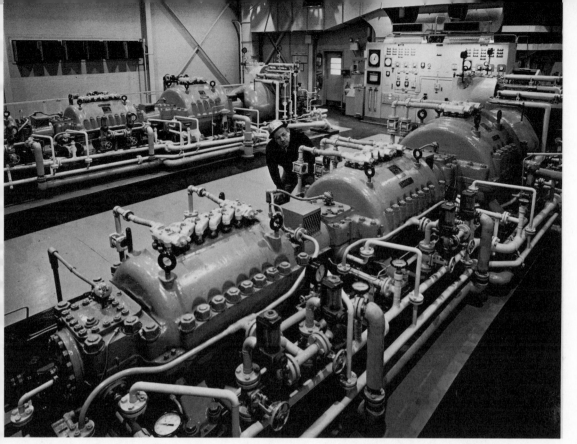

With his high purchasing power, the average American worker can buy and use a large share of industry's products, thereby shaping the prosperity of the whole nation. More important, he is protected from the fear of poverty by social security funds, unemployment insurance, accident and health benefits, and job security. Many older problems have been solved, but new ones emerge. One in four Americans are still considered impoverished and an anti-poverty campaign is underway in all states to close the gap, as we shall see in a later chapter.

Chrysler Corp.

CHAPTER 3

AUTOMATION: A NEW LOOK AT MAN AND HIS WORK

The ax was the caveman's passport out of the world of beasts. The Industrial Revolution took the back-breaking toil and monotonous repetition out of jobs, making possible shorter working days, better pay, and more time for learning and leisure. Within the last decade, new types of machines have come into use — computers and process control equipment. Automation has brought the twentieth century into the world of magic. Like all works of the imagination, the rapid speed of change fills us with wonder and bewilderment. Space scientists no longer speak of *if* but *when* they will land men on the moon, thanks to computer technology. Leaping from "Maybe I'll try it," to "How did I ever do without it?" we take dial telephones and orbiting artronauts for granted. Automation has contributed many miracles to the range of production, distribution, and consumption — not alone in the United States but also in many other countries.

Self-run machines assemble ingredients or parts; alter, adapt, measure, and combine them; check on their work for error and correct it; then slow down, speed up, or vary production according to the moment's need. The machines produce, assemble, wrap products, and deliver them ready for market with a minimum of help from human hands. Then, there are the machines that can "compute," "think," even make decisions at lightning speed.

Automation has led to tremendous changes in the work skills needed to carry on efficient production. Computers have created new products, new industries, and new jobs. They are extending the possibility of human knowledge and are opening new vistas for research into education, health, and sociology, which will help promote greater conservation of human resources.

This chapter brings into focus some of the problems that have arisen from automation. In some industries, workers have been automated out of jobs; elsewhere, there is a shortage of workers with a basic education who can be trained for the computer age.

Where possible, workers are being retrained or encouraged to retire at an earlier age. For young people, the message is clear. A basic high school education, or more, can open the door to jobs that were unknown to their parents and grandparents, jobs unknown even today.

We cannot curb man's will to invent new devices and create new products. We can only hope that he has the will and power to use his inventions for human betterment.

Automation All Around

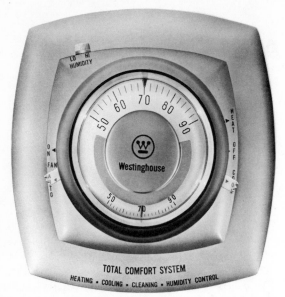

You wake up on a cold morning to the sound of a radio pre-set to turn itself on by an attached clock. The room is heated to a comfortable temperature. You wash with warm water that has a controlled temperature. You eat toast — browned to your liking, drink orange juice kept cold in the refrigerator, or coffee that has been percolated and kept

hot on an electric appliance. The heater, toaster, refrigerator, coffee maker were all regulated by thermostats, one of the basic inventions of the automated age.

A thermostat is a small device that controls temperature. It is made of a substance that expands when heated and contracts when cooled. For example, if an electric iron should reach a pre-set degree of heat, the expansion of the metal would cause the thermostat to cut off the electric

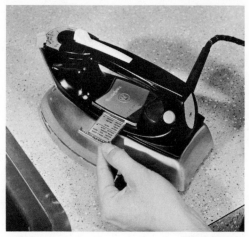

current. The temperature would cool and, before it got too cold, the thermostat would cause the current to go on once more. In other words, one type of mechanical device is used to control other mechanical devices. There are many kinds of thermostats and hundreds of ways in which they are used. This single invention has helped design machines that can perform pre-set tasks alone or in series in a self-directing, self-correcting fashion.

Warm-blooded animals have a kind of thermostat built into their bodies which keeps the temperature inside the body at an even heat, even

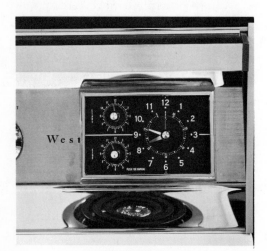

Westinghouse

The human nervous system and brain control a sequence of operations which engineers try to imitate in automated machines. The machines have their "hardware" made of metal, plastic, wires, and electrical parts to resemble the physical structure of the body. They need also the "software" of human inventive genius to design, program, and operate them. As we examine such machines on the following pages, the physical, muscle-joint operations may be considered the workers; the power system function resembles the foreman, and the mechanical brain is a kind of manager.

though the temperature outside may be higher or lower. In fact, the human body guards many secrets of automation which engineers and scientists are trying to imitate. The food we eat moves in an orderly manner, at a uniform speed, from the mouth through the digestive organs, each equipped with fluids and chemicals that act upon the food. The food is broken down and changed to a variety of products, each intended for use by different parts of the body. How does some food become tissue, some blood, some bone, some waste? The entire digestive process is automated and pre-set to produce predictable end-products. More than that, the body corrects itself when there is too much food, gives warning when there is a breakdown in the "machinery," and sends signals when the supply runs low.

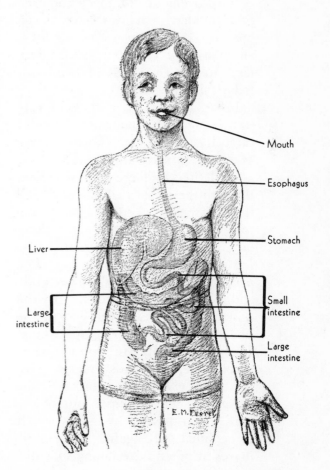

Mouth

Esophagus

Stomach

Liver

Small intestine

Large intestine

Large intestine

E. M. Freret

Thomas Nelson and Sons, E. M. Freret.

The Automated Worker

Young Dagwood in the comic strip was famous for his enormous appetite. Late at night he would sneak into the kitchen, line up a pile of bread slices and raid the refrigerator. Meat, cheese, eggs and jelly; then pickles, mustard, and relish would be piled between the bread slices, and Dagwood managed to consume it all before our eyes.

Huge machines, like Dagwood, have a capacity to consume quantities of materials. Maybe the Dagwood appetites caused baking to be taken out of the home, out of small bake shops, and into huge factories with enormous ovens. After years of improvements to meet competition, modern bakeries have developed the baking process as one long, automatic march from raw ingredients to the final loaf of bread for today's Dagwoods.

Flour, eggs, milk, and other substances, fed into enormous vats in carefully controlled portions are blended, mixed, and kneaded for a fixed time by large blades. Then, through these vats a ribbon of dough flows at measured speed into grease-sprayed pans. The pans move along on a conveyor belt, each pan receiving its allotted share of dough. The pans are shaken gently as they glide and the dough begins to rise. By the time the pans reach the end of the line, the dough is ready for baking. Into a moving oven they go and, after a set time, the pans emerge with loaves of gold-crusted bread. The loaves are gently tapped out of the pans which proceed by conveyor belt to be filled once again. Meanwhile, loaves of bread move along to a slic-

ing machine, a wrapping machine, a sealing machine, and to waiting trucks.

The steps in sifting, pouring, kneading, shaping, snipping the dough, the baking, the slicing, cutting, wrapping and sealing are performed automatically, swiftly, and efficiently. This system also assures cleanliness and uniform quality. The machines do more — they can correct errors along the way and avoid unnecessary delay or faulty products.

This kind of automation finds application in many other industries in which machines are used to run other machines. Ammonia, oil, and other liquids are pumped over long distances from source to consumer and, along the way, they may be changed to different substances. Oil is pumped from the well through pipelines in an uninterrupted stream. At pumping stations along the way, the oil is pushed forward or re-directed to a special processing plant. The oil is heated, purified, mixed, separated, and altered by chemicals or pressure through automated processing. Some of the oil is changed to gasoline, some to heating or fuel oil, some to raw materials from which plastics are made.

In spite of the machine operations in the oil industry, automation did not really take the place of human labor. By greatly increasing the productivity of oil and helping to conserve the natural supply, automation eliminated wasteful processes, lowered prices of oil products, increased consumption; new industries were made possible and large numbers of workers were employed.

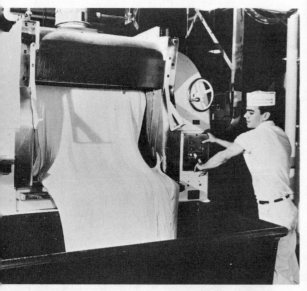

All Photos courtesy:
Continental Baking Co.
National Biscuit Co.

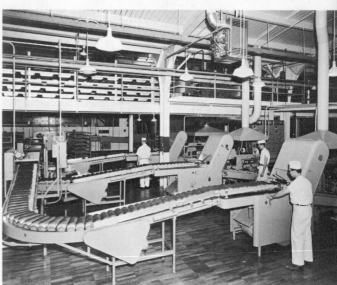

The Automated Foreman

Charlie Chaplin, the great film comedian, lived through an automation nightmare in the movie, *Modern Times*. Strapped and helpless, he was used to demonstrate an automatic feeding machine. Somehow, the machine went berserk and moved faster and faster, out of control, jamming endless scoops of stew, potatoes, and pie between his jaws, as coffee flooded his eyes, nose, and ears.

Can you imagine an unmanned n e e d l e factory where tons and mountains of needles are turned out — all without eyes? Or egg-shaped wheels produced by mistake; or a doughnut-making machine that never stops, as in the story, *Homer Price* by Robert McCloskey?

How do machines prevent such breakdowns? Who's to mind the store? For such situations, machines have a built-in "foreman" that checks for error and even corrects the error without interruption. At certain stages in the operation, a machine has an inspection mechanism that checks for size, weight, shape, texture. In the manufacture of buttons, for example, the buttons pass along a series of slots that reject imperfect buttons and throw them off the moving belt.

Through such operations, the manufacture or refining of products may go on for months, even years, wtihout interruption — except for maintenance or repair of the machinery. Hours of monotonous drudgery are thus spared the workers and larger quantities of goods can be produced in less time at lower cost. The result has been a shift in the kinds of jobs that can be performed in industry — jobs that demand an adequate education and the ability to change as the demands change.

The railroad signalman in the picture checks with the computer controls that slow down the speed of cars by causing other machines, called retarders, to work.

Louisville and Nashville R.R.

In the production of photographic film, automatic controls operate the different stages of processing. If a signal light should show a maladjustment, an operator can correct the condition by remote control.

Without automation, much of the research on atomic energy would have been impossible. The Cosmotron at Brookhaven National Laboratory in Long Island, New York accelerates protons in a circular path to speeds approaching the velocity of light with an energy of 3 billion electron volts. Automated equipment, aided by heavy concrete shielding blocks, guides scientists in their studies.

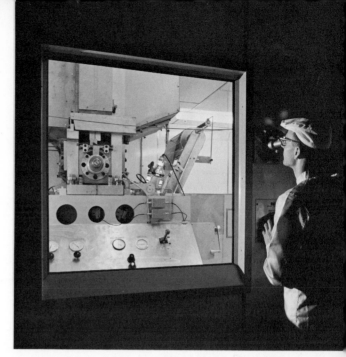

DuPont

Brookhaven National Laboratory

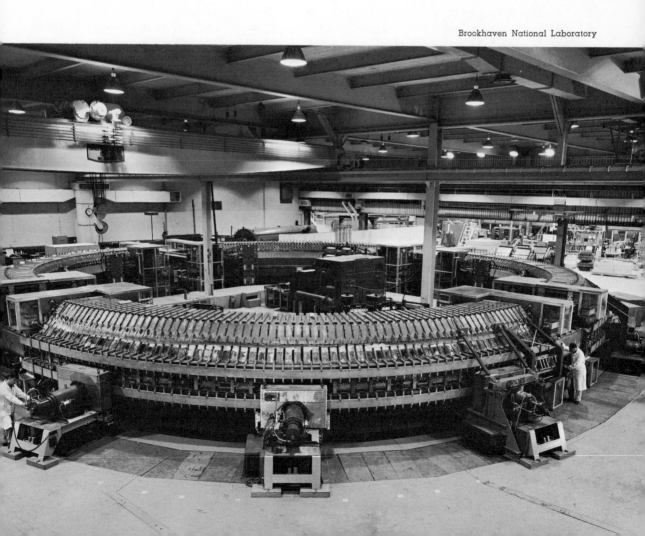

Feedback

The mechanism inside a machine that helps to control a change from the normal is called the feedback. Here is how it works in the body. If you begin to feel ill, your body has sent out a warning. If you go to bed and rest, the chances are that you will begin to feel better. But often you want to know more about your condition so you put your body to an inspection test by checking your temperature. If the thermometer reading is above normal, you have a fever and proceed to correct the condition by taking aspirin and hobbling off to bed.

Mothers use feedback, too. When a housewife tastes her cooking and finds it too bland, she corrects the condition by adding salt, pepper, or other spices. Machines are built with similar correcting devices, the feedback. When salad oil is produced in a factory, spices and oil are mixed in pre-set quantities. Should there be too much salt, instruments will detect it, the salt-flow valve will adjust itself, and the mixture is then corrected to its proper proportions. Feedback is the secret of uniformity in products, a kind of guarantee that the "foreman" has checked the quality of the merchandise and the feedback has made any needed corrections.

One of the earliest kinds of feedback was an attachment to a windmill, some 200 years ago in Holland. Since a windmill depends for its movement on variable winds, there are times when it cannot operate. The new device was a small windmill set on the turret at right angles to the main mill. This mill would catch the winds that the large mill might miss, and its whirling motion would swing the turret around on its track and cause the large mill to go into action. The small mill, away from the wind, was again ready to go into action as the wind shifted.

A great breakthrough for inventors came with the harnessing of steam power. As early as 1788, James Watt designed a self-regulating throttle to control the flow of steam into his steam engine. First wind, then steam, then electricity, and now electromagnetism — all have been used in the feedback operation.

One of the first automated machines was the Jacquard loom. Invented in France early in the 1800's, it was used to weave floral designs in cloth. In this process, the design is transferred to punched-hole patterns on paper and the yarn made to pass through the holes in the desired pattern. There is a perforation opposite each needle. As the cylinder is pressed down, the needles to be used for the design pass through the holes; the others are blocked. When the cylinder moves up, all the needles are restored to their original position. The punched cards are perforated by a special machine from a painted design.

The player-piano, based on the use of air pressure through perforated paper, transmits sounds from a roll of punched paper moving around a drum to the piano keys, note for note and chord for chord.

The punched-tape principle is applied to the production of different

A player-piano roll.

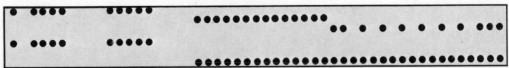

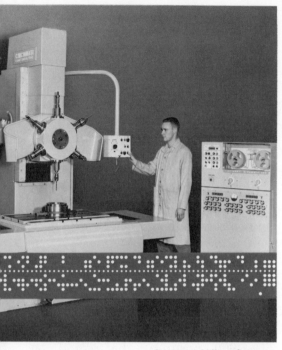

Ford Motor Company

An eight-cylinder engine block is bored
by automated equipment.

Cincinnati Milling Company

A computer-controlled turret drill and a
sample of the punched tape.

kinds of tools and machine parts.
The tools to be made are put into a
code on the tape, which is attached
to the machine. An operator places
a piece of metal on the bed of the
machine and turns a switch. The
machine begins an elaborate process
which may move the operation
through several machines. Not only
does the punched tape control the
production of a variety of products,
but the tapes can be stored for re-
use at any time with a record of materials used and number of items
produced.

Automation may be illustrated
through the production of engine
blocks in the auto industry. The engine block is a metal case containing
a series of holes. When it arrives as
a rough iron casting from the foun-
dry, it needs 617 different operations
performed on 22 different machines.
In 38 seconds, one machine performs
105 of these operations; another machine can perform work on 17 blocks
at once. The engine blocks are
moved automatically from one group
of machines to another with preci-
sion timing. At some time during
the operations, men at an assembly
line install pistons, connect rods, or
do other jobs. Mechanical arms overhead hold the blocks in place and
move them along to the next operation.

As a result of these time-saving
operations, it now takes 150 hours
to produce a car, half as long as it
took a generation ago. The output
of car manufacturing has increased
because automation has accelerated
the amount of work that can be
done by the same number of or
fewer workers.

The Automated Brain -- The Manager

Punched cards were the first automated system of record-keeping. The system grew out of the needs of the United States Census Bureau in 1885. While the country was willingly receiving large numbers of immigrants to swell the labor ranks, the rate was too rapid for the census takers. Dr. Herman Hollerith, a statistician at the Bureau, had nightmares because he thought the Bureau would still be counting the population figures for 1890 when the 1900 period rolled around. Borrowing the principle of the Jacquard loom, he organized figures on punched card patterns. He recorded the census data on a long strip of paper, punched holes in a planned pattern so that each hole in a specific place meant a specific thing. He used a special machine to examine the holes electrically and added the desired information. Later, cards of a special size and thickness replaced the paper.

Punch-card machines are now used in thousands of ways. School systems can quickly sort out all the children born in May of a certain year, or all those who had received a passing mark in a national examination, and so on. Insurance companies, social security offices, railroads, department stores, all use punch-card sorting machines. The card shown here is $7\frac{3}{8}''$ x $3\frac{1}{4}''$, of a thickness that must be exactly the right type for the sorting operations. There are 80 vertical areas or columns, numbered at the bottom. Each card has 12 punching positions, giving 960 positions that could be marked for different kinds of information. Cards are stacked for sorting according to the corner cut. They may also be arranged by different colors.

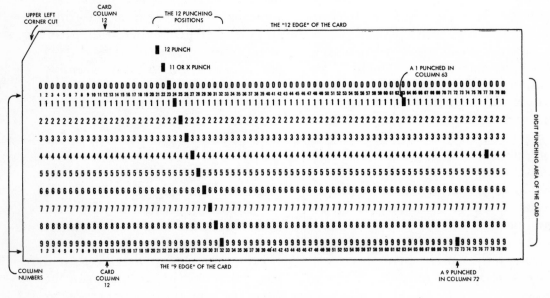

IBM

A typical punch card.

Information stored on punched cards is available over long periods of time, to be used for different purposes. When a specific kind of information is sought, the cards are passed through a machine that "reads" the holes and converts them into electrical impulses of varying duration, depending upon the code. When the cards have been sorted and "read," the impulses are processed and the results may emerge as a printed line or new holes punched in each card. The sorting machine moves very quickly, at speeds of 450 to 2,000 cards per minute, dropping the cards into separate pockets, according to the information on the twelve punching positions.

IBM

A card sorting machine.

This machine can "read" 800 cards a minute; the data then goes to the processing unit for computation and storage on magnetic tape, shown at right.

IBM

Information Retrieval

Computers fed by coded cards, paper, or magnetic tape perform miracles of exactness in many areas of knowledge. They prepare complicated chemical formulas, analyze processes, predict voting or marketing trends, keep an ongoing inventory of materials, make nationwide, accurate airplane reservations, and carry out many other important operations. Computers work with units too tiny or too large for the mind to cope with; they work at intervals of time too slow or too rapid to handle. Technicians talk of microseconds (a thousandth of a second), or even nanoseconds (a billionth of a second) in calculating processes.

Beyond carrying out these remarkable mental operations, computers store the answers for later use in thousands of combinations. This is the great advantage of automated devices — their capacity for information retrieval.

Data-processing computers deal with numbers. They are like robot accountants working at lightning speed. They compute complicated mathematical problems, make instantaneous changes, store information, and provide an ongoing record of facts and figures.

Computers may vary according to the manufacturer, but they all contain a kind of input device, a processing unit, a storage unit, and a kind of output device. Coded information (known as a program) is recorded on cards, paper tape, magnetic tape, or on paper in magnetic ink. The same machine, almost at once, begins to type out answers at a speed much greater than the one typed by the human operator because it operates electronically.

Information that is fed into a computer (programed) is translated into a very simple code. For example, the code may be the placement of zeros and ones in a predetermined order, known as the binary system. This system was used to transmit pictures from Mariner IV on its flight to Mars in July, 1965.

The still pictures taken by the Mariner camera were scanned and broken into 64 different shades of gray. Each shade became a number, and the numbers were transmitted to the tracking station in NASA's Jet Propulsion Laboratory. The signals were amplified, taped, and fed into computers. Each sequence of 6 "zeros" and "ones" became a piece of visual information, which was then reconverted into one of the 64 shades of gray to make a picture, much like the tiny dots that make up the picture on a home TV screen.

Although data processing machines work automatically, they really depend upon program analysts, engineers, and many other people who design, program, and operate them. More important, it is for people to make the decisions based on information provided by the computers.

Computers are already at work in the service of humanity. The possibilities for the future are unending. Vast amounts of data can be fed and stored for use in planning ways of improving living and working conditions of people all over the world. Thus, inventions born to serve industry and government are once again applied to serve mankind in a variety of ways.

NASA

NASA

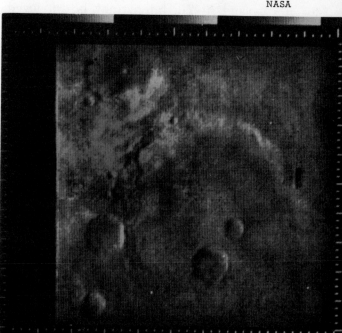

Conducting Business By Computer

As business operations have grown in complexity, data processing has helped to meet the changing pace. For example, banks had to find an economical way of processing 10 billion checks each day when it was realized that each check had to be handled six times from deposit to cancellation. The American Bankers Association, working with computer manufacturers, instituted a system of magnetic character sensing on checks. When you look at a check blank, you will see a strange set of characters and numerals. The code on the check contains information about the bank of origin, the depositor's account number, and other data. A bank clerk need only add the amount in magnetic print when the check returns to the bank of origin, and the check is processed at once. This system makes possible the processing of 70,000 checks per hour, if necessary. Bank balances for individual depositors are printed at 20 lines per second. No wonder the prediction is that all purchasing may some day be paid by check.

Not only is data quickly processed and stored, but it may be retrieved

Consolidated Edison

Reading a customer's account in 20 seconds.

at great speed and transmitted over long distances by teletype. The computer, together with microfilm records, serves telephone, electric or gas companies and department stores with efficiency.

To answer an inquiry from a customer, the operator selects the roll of film on which the customer's account is recorded, finds the proper frame on his microfilm reader, inquires of the on-line c o m p u t e r whether recent changes have been made on the record, and views the information on his video screen. The entire operation may take only 20 seconds. This service is available for millions of customers.

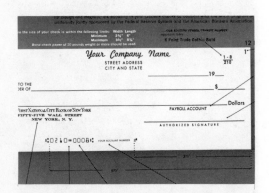

A coded check imprinted with magnetic ink.

In the stockroom of a factory, two-way "conversations" can be carried on between the computer and the sales or accounting office. The operator types out information about the inventory in his stockpile; in turn, he receives shipping orders and inventory checklists from any of the offices.

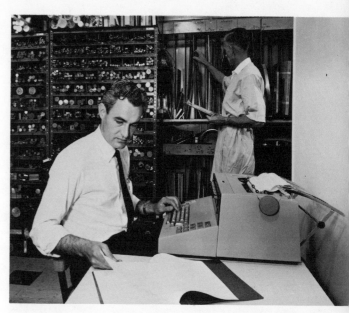

Keeping a continual inventory in the stockroom by data communications.

The teletyped information seen in the foreground of the picture on the right can be exchanged among 200 terminals of the Air Force Combat Logistics Network. Data is translated into code on punched card, paper tape, or printed form by the computers seen in the background and stored in the control panel. At command, the most recent information may be sent by teleprinter to any or all of the terminals.

Computers are still very costly and require special training in their use. A single computer may cost about a quarter of a million dollars, ranging in price from $50,000 to $3,000,000. That is why many firms rent the equipment and engage specialists to help prepare materials for their special needs. Like other inventions in the past, the cost of producing and operating computers will decline as the demand increases.

Air Force Combat Logistics Terminal.

The Changing World Of Work

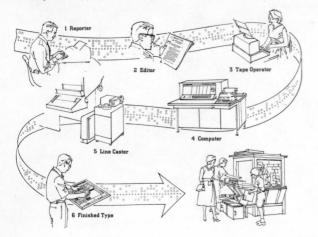

IBM 1620 Type Composition

1 Reporter
2 Editor
3 Tape Operator
4 Computer
5 Line Caster
6 Finished Type

IBM

During the first 200 years of its development, the United States was an agricultural land. Most jobs were related to farming, with a smaller proportion in trade, manufacturing, and services. The Industrial Revolution changed the balance, and the nation needed more factory and industrial workers and f e w e r farm

NASA

workers. Among the non-farm workers, however, most were "blue-collar" workers, that is, they were engaged in physical labor rather than in office or sales jobs. The 20th century saw a great drop in the demand for farm and mine workers and a shift in the proportion of goods-producing jobs to service industry jobs.

For example, 53% of the jobs in 1945 were in goods-producing industries and 47% in trade, transportation, public utilities, finance, real estate, sales, repairs, and other services. These are more likely to be "white-collar" jobs. In 1960, the service industries had risen to make up 55% of the work force, and by 1970 it is estimated that there will be a still greater difference between the number of service jobs and goods-producing jobs.

What does this trend mean to young people now at school? It suggests that they will have a better chance to earn a living in service industries than in farming, mining or manufacturing. It also means that they need a basic education — high school graduation or more — with an understanding of mathematics, mechanics, economics, business management, office skills, and reading comprehension. Workers in the future will need to be able to change from one kind of work to another, through additional education or re-training. There will be plenty of opportunity for advancement up the economic ladder for qualified and ambitious men and women. "There is no room at the bottom," is the advice of the vocational counselors.

The future outlook for older workers with limited skills and for unskilled blue-collar workers is not as encouraging. It is estimated that some two million people are displaced each year by labor-saving inventions. Workers in the railroad, printing, shipping, and other industries are concerned about their jobs. They point to the coal industry as an example of what is in store for them, unless long-range plans are made now. Coal miners accepted the use of machines because these took the drudgery out of their work and greatly increased their safety. But, as a result, tens of thousands of men were automated out of jobs, unable to find new ones. It takes only 125,000 miners to do the work once performed by 500,000 men.

Workers, threatened with the loss of jobs, and management, intent upon increasing efficiency to reduce costs, would appear to be at opposite sides of the question. But men of good will representing management, labor, and government are trying to find compromise plans that would permit greater mechanization, reduce costs and the size of the work force, meet competition, and still k e e p employment rates and the standard of living high.

NEA

The Shifting Patterns of Employment

TOTAL CIVILIAN EMPLOYMENT (PERCENT)

	1929	1964
MINING	2.6	1.0
FINANCE, INSURANCE AND REAL ESTATE	3.6	4.7
CONTRACT CONSTRUCTION	3.6	4.9
TRANSPORTATION AND PUBLIC UTILITIES	9.4	6.3
AGRICULTURE	25.0	7.6
SERVICE AND MISCELLANEOUS		13.6
GOVERNMENT	8.2	15.3
WHOLESALE AND RETAIL TRADE	7.3	19.3
NONDURABLE GOODS	14.7	11.8
TOTAL MANUFACTURING		
DURABLE GOODS	25.8	15.6

1929 1935 1940 1945 1950 1955 1960 1964

White-Collar Jobs Up; Blue-Collar Jobs Down

TOTAL CIVILIAN EMPLOYMENT (PERCENT)

WHITE-COLLAR / BLUE-COLLAR

	1947	1964	1975
FARM WORKERS	14	7	4
SERVICE WORKERS	10	13	14
SALES	5	6	7
PROFESSIONAL	8	12	15
MANAGERS AND OFFICIALS	10	11	10
CLERICAL	12	15	17
LABORERS (EXCEPT FARM)	7	5	4
CRAFTSMEN AND FOREMEN	13	13	13
OPERATIVES	21	18	17

WHITE-COLLAR: 35 (1964: 44, 1975: 48)
BLUE-COLLAR: 41 (1964: 36, 1975: 34)

1947 1950 1955 1960 1964 1975

CHAPTER 4

EDUCATION IN THE AMERICAN TRADITION

Education has been one of the main concerns of the American people since the beginning of their history. The Northwest Ordinance of 1787 stated it in this fashion: " Religion, morality, and knowledge being necessary to good government and the happiness of mankind, schools and the means of education shall forever be encouraged." Free public schools were established in all the territories thereafter, and as each territory became a state, the tradition of free public education continued.

Immigrants who came to settle and work in our new land represented a variety of ethnic groups, each speaking a different language, having differences in traditions, customs, and religious beliefs. The public schools helped to blend the best of the old and the new, and transformed their children into Americans — vital and capable builders of a great nation.

At first, the educational dream was modest — just enough schooling to prepare a young man or woman for making a living on a farm or in a trade. A secondary school education or college graduation were available mainly to the upper classes, in the European tradition. As science and invention increased man's range of knowledge, more schooling was needed for the mass of people. Boys and girls had to acquire new skills for the machine age. With a growing middle class, parents sought a better education for their children. Elementary school graduation became compulsory for children in all states and high school graduation in most. Today, at least half of all young people go on to college.

The question may be asked, how much education is enough, and why should it be extended to so many? There are no limits to education for our time and we must accept the fact that education goes on "from the cradle to the grave." The reasons are many. We can never really finish learning all there is to know, especially when new knowledge is being added at a dizzying pace. We also need ongoing education to meet ever-changing demands in employment. We must learn how to understand and act on problems that face the family, community, state, region, and nation. We must learn how to use our ever increasing leisure hours. Education is the answer for each individual.

It is also the answer for the nation. One of the best investments a nation can make is in the education of its people. Today, after long years of inequalities in educational opportunity, the United States is involved in one of the greatest educational programs of all time. As early as 1947, a Commission on Education appointed by President Harry S. Truman recommended:

"Education is an investment, not a cost. It is an investment in free men . . . in social welfare, better living standards, better health, and less crime . . . in higher production, increased income . . .
It is an investment in a bulwark against garbled information, half-truths and untruths; against ignorance and intolerance . . . It is an investment in human talent, better human relationships, democracy and peace."

U. S. Dept. of Agri.

Progress In Four Generations

"Poor boy to millionaire" has been a familiar theme in American stories. We read about the Rockefellers and Carnegies, knowing that their achievements are true but rare. The greater inspiration comes from the countless numbers of families whose children rose within a few generations from the ranks of uneducated immigrant toilers to skilled crafts-

Statue of Liberty. With six carefully hoarded dollars and only the clothes on his back, he faced an uncertain future. In his native Poland, Andrew had been an unskilled farm-hand, unable to eke out a bare living from long hours of work. In America, he hoped to shape a better life.

Andrew landed in New York and went to Pittsburgh where he had rel-

Lewis Hine photo

Ford Motor Company

men, business men, members of the professions, and statesmen. This is the dream of the fair chance which caused families to leave their class-locked societies where there was little opportunity for a man to become whatever was best in him.

Take the Stuchko family as an example. Fifty years ago, undernourished and miserable in a crowded steamship, Andrew Stuchko counted the days as the vessel neared the

atives. He was put to work in a dreary, unsafe coal mine. But Andrew was not disillusioned; the hope inside him still burned brightly and he worked hard. He was determined that his sons would have the opportunities he had missed.

They did. Young John had eight years of free schooling. It made his parents proud to listen when he read them the daily newspaper. John left the mining city and went to work on a Detroit auto assembly line. He was more highly paid than his father, had shorter work days in a clean, safe factory. Still, John planned an even better life for his children. They would not have to spend hours at monotonous, repetitious tasks. Learning was the key.

So John encouraged his son, Peter, to stay on and complete his high

Stuchko lived to see his dream come true. Dr. Andrew Stuchko, great-grandson of an illiterate immigrant, no longer needed to spend hours at backbreaking work w h e r e only brawn, not brains, was used.

The story of the Stuchko family is an example of the American policy of an Open Society, in which each individual can go as far as his energy

Standard Oil Co. (N.J.)

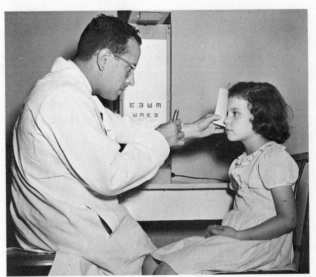

U. S. Public Health Service

school education. Peter had a way with machinery. He could look at a mechanical breakdown and make repairs using his own talent and his knowledge of mathematics and mechanics. Peter had a skill that was useful for his time, and he became a successful machinist. It was his son, Andrew Stuchko, Jr., who finally climbed higher on the ladder of success. He was able to go to college and medical school. At last, old Andrew

and ability can take him. This is in contrast to the Closed Society, in which the individual is born into and must remain on the land in a fixed occupation or social class. Although the succeeding generations of Stuchkos may have had no greater intelligence at birth than their great-grandfather, they did have the opportunity to develop according to their desires and interests, and to achieve a better standard of living.

The Mind Of Man

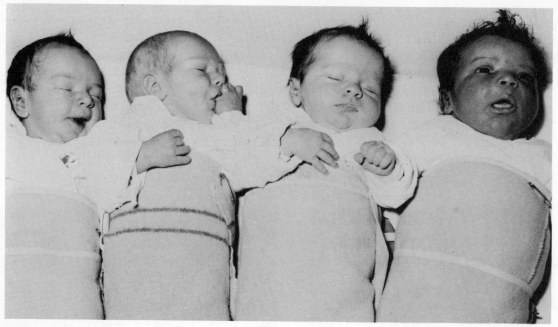

Kitrosser for UNESCO

The animal knows — but only man knows that he knows! What is this gift that makes man supreme in nature? It lies in the brain, the organ which gives man the capacity to learn, to remember, and to create. Each individual human infant has an unlimited capacity to learn. Just how much and in what way he can be helped to learn best is the subject of a great deal of research.

The brain is an organ, weighing about three pounds. It contains about 10 billion nerve cells that look like a pleated mass of gray and white matter. Each cell maintains an average of more than 10,000 connections with other cells or neurons. The brain is capable of more connections — between ideas and knowledge, or skills and memory — than four times the population of the earth.

Central sections of the brain control special functions. One section regulates seeing, another hearing, speaking, and so on. Other sections integrate the senses so that we see, hear, and touch at the same time. Still other parts control thinking, memory, and emotions. The brain is able to receive all stimuli that come from the eyes, ears, taste buds, etc. It stores impressions for later use and it

performs instantaneous connections to tell us what we are seeing, hearing, or tasting or to help us make decisions.

The brain's operations are more complicated than a telephone hook-up among all the people of the world. Moreover, the messages pass with lightning speed from one path to another, and never in exactly the same way. No computer yet devised is as complicated as the working of the brain. The highways of communication are based in the spinal cord, from which a network of nerve fibers or threads radiate. All our actions are carried on by the brain and nervous system through chemical and electrical activity. Scientists are carrying on complicated research to try to fathom how the human mind works.

Should anyone attempt to design a working model of the human brain, he would learn that it consists of billions of different cells. He would have to reconstruct each cell with its intricate chemical and physical matter, intercellular material, and trigger mechanism. If he could compress a cell into a quarter-inch cube, he would have to prepare 10 billion more. He would need a place large enough to hold the total of 1½ cubic feet of cells. In order to trace the electrical impulses that move through the nerve cells, he would have to wire the cells at a cost that would be 10 million times the national debt. So faint is the electrical discharge of each cell, that 60,000 scalps together might supply enough electricity to light a flashbulb. The imitation brain would need one million kilowatts of electric power, whereas the brain actually uses only 25 kilowatts.

Each human being has the capacity to learn. Not only does he learn to take care of his needs — as do the other forms of animal life — but he can change his behavior according to the conditions. He has learned to use language with which he can interpret ideas and imagine endless new ones.

How far can newborn babies go in life? That will depend upon their native ability, their own desire to learn, and the opportunities available to them. American education aims to serve every child in our society, each to his own ability.

Learning From An Early Age

Wausau Schools

Lower forms of animal life depend upon inborn ways of behaving, or instincts. They move through life doing things — finding food, building a nest, caring for young — exactly as their instincts dictate. Human babies have few instincts. Human infants, however, have a tremendous capacity for learning, and a boundless curiosity to find out. Watch a small child trying to find his place in his young world. He asks innumerable questions and remembers the answers. The wonder is that so small a child can learn with such amazing sureness; the pity is that, as he grows older, he seems to lose the joy of inquiry and his pace of learning slows down.

Scientists tell us that the average, well-informed adult uses less than five per cent of his brain capacity. They tell us that any normal individual can be helped to learn abstract ideas if he has the desire to do so and if he understands the reason why.

Before a child enters school, his learning is informal. It comes from the people and the things about him. Children who have been loved, taken on outings, who have engaged in conversations with grownups and with other children, who have had stories

Standard Oil Co. (N.J.)

U. S. Dept. of Agri.

Engelberg for OEO

read to them, have looked at pictures and have watched children's programs on television acquire a great deal of knowledge before they come to school.

American children start school when they are five years old, though compulsory education does not begin until they are six years old. Parents who can afford to pay for early schooling sometimes send children to a nursery school or pre-kindergarten. It has now become evident that chil-

dren from a deprived cultural environment need schooling before they reach the age of five, if they are to catch up with more fortunate children. Through grants from private foundations and government sources, three and four-year-olds are now going to school to receive a "head start" for later learning. Thus, when they arrive at kindergarten or first grade, these children will be ready for reading and writing and speaking.

M. Engelberg for OEO

School Is Where You Find It

Long before you start to go to school your education has begun. You learn from parents, relatives and neighbors; from children your own age, older, or even younger; from people you meet in shops and on the street.

When you notice something new, your mind organizes bits and pieces of information — recalls from the storehouse of memory what you already knew, adds the new information to it, and changes what you knew to new ideas. We call this process *learning*. By observing, reasoning, thinking, inquiring, dreaming, imagining, and creating you are learning, just as surely as you are breathing. There is no end to learning; it takes place from the moment of birth and continues throughout life.

Monkmeyer

You learn to take turns.

There are all kinds of opportunities for learning. School is the most important source of knowledge because it provides an environment for learning u n d e r the direction of

You learn by watching animals at the zoo.

N. Y. City Park Dept.

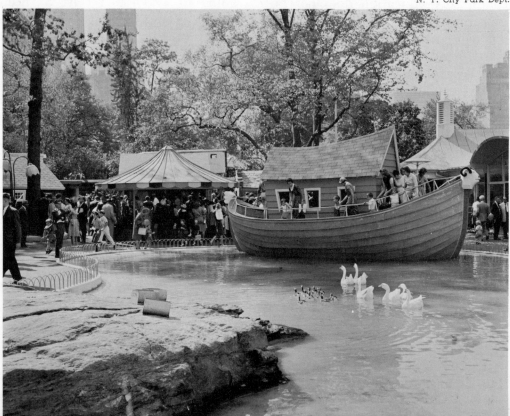

Worchester Art Museum, Massachusetts.

You learn when the family takes you to the museum.

trained teachers. But, there are many other "schools" from which to learn.

You learn from visits to museums, libraries, zoos, botanical gardens. You learn when you play, when you watch people at work, or when you take part in community affairs. You learn by observing natural phenomena just outside the door — changes in weather and what happens to puddles and hillsides when it storms; changes in the seasons when trees, flowers, and animals take on new shapes and colors. You learn from travel to places near and far. You learn from television, newspapers, magazines. All you need then to become educated is to look, listen, and learn.

Boy Scouts of America

You learn with friends.

U. S. Dept of Agri.

You learn by team play.

A team of second graders carry out an experiment.

Education for all the children of all the people — the American tradition. For nearly 300 years this goal has been sought, but never before has it been so close to being achieved.

Let's examine this principle, step by step. What do we mean by *education*? What constitutes a good education? How do people learn? How do they learn best? Parents and educators keep asking these questions and trying to find answers. Here are some of the goals of education as they have been expressed over many gen-

So much to learn . . . .

erations. Which ones do you agree with?

Education is learning to read, write, and figure.

Education is for the aristocracy — it is learning morals, manners, art, literature, music.

Education is a preparation for life — how to become a carpenter, draftsman, chemist, typist.

Education is learning science, mathematics, engineering, medicine, accountancy.

Education is history, geography, literature — and all of the other things put together.

Education is learning how to learn and how to keep on learning in a wide variety of subjects.

Philadelphia School District

Civic action in junior high school.

Ford Foundation

New arrivals from Cuba join the language arts class.

A serious discussion in a social studies class.

Learning to use business machines in high school.

What about *"the education of all the children?"* There are children who are slow to learn abstract ideas and complicated skills; those who learn much more quickly than others and need to be challenged; those who are reluctant to learn at all. There are children who are physically, emotionally, and mentally different from most other children. Can they all be educated? Those who are concerned with education say they can, and to help them succeed they draw upon the experience of experts in medicine, psychology, sociology, law, religion, and many other fields.

Finally, education is conceived as the responsibility of the community to all the people in all social and economic and political levels of society. As you look at these pictures of children at school, how well do you think we are teaching all the children of all the people?

Philadelphia School District

Music is part of education.

City children learn about farming firsthand.

Battle Creek, Michigan

The American Tradition

An engraving of Harvard College, by Paul Revere, 1767.

University Hall, Harvard as it looks now.

American education, since the beginning of our history, has been provided by local communities under the direction of each state government. This is in contrast to most other countries of the world in which national departments of education operate and regulate the educational system. The American system stems from a fear that federal support would mean federal control or autocracy.

University of Virginia established by Thomas Jefferson.

The earliest Massachusetts colonists, facing problems of survival against a hostile climate, terrain, and Indian natives, wrote provisions for free schooling into their first set of laws. In 1789, a school law required the establishment of an elementary school in each town with 50 or more families and a high school in each town with 150 or more families. Pennsylvania, North Carolina, New Hampshire, Vermont, and other colonies passed similar laws. New York had a keen interest in education, but it did not pass an official law for free education until 1894.

Colonial education was influenced by the ideas of Thomas Jefferson, who said, "If a nation expects to be ignorant and free in a state of civilization, it expects what never was and never will be." But Jefferson believed in the education of all white children for three years, with further education reserved only for the very bright. In his time, however, children had other educational influences. They learned skills from par-

Nursing students, Alaska Junior College.

A mathematics lecture, University of Chicago.

ents and craftsmen; they learned politics firsthand. Compulsory education for at least five years was established early in America's history, but for rural children, especially Negro rural children, this education was very scant.

Colleges for qualified young people were established at the time of settlement. Harvard College was established in 1636. Yale, Dartmouth, Brown, and other colleges were built before the American Revolution. For 200 years, most college education was privately sponsored.

The federal government gave very little support to education until 1862, when the Morrill Act was passed. Income from federal "land grants," as well as outright subsidies, financed the training of young people for agriculture, mechanical arts, and military science. The 97 land-grant colleges throughout the nation still offer free or low-cost education to young people of every race, creed, or economic level, some 30% of all students attending college.

After World War II, a "G. I. Education Bill" gave scholarships and maintenance grants to young men whose education had been interrupted by the war. At least a million veterans took advantage of this law, and the policy has since been continued for all service men, even those who have not been in service in wartime.

Because medical training is so costly, there is a shortage of schools and doctors.

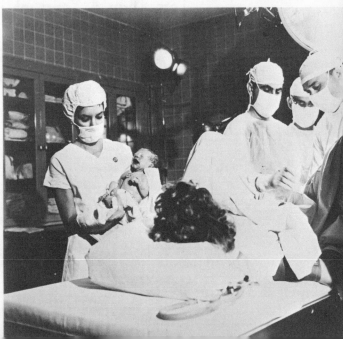

Equalizing Educational Opportunity

Although education is, in theory, available to all the children, it became clear by 1964 that there were great gaps in the quality of education that hundreds of thousands of children were receiving. Many school districts could not afford the growing cost of school construction, well-trained teachers, and instructional materials necessary for a good educational system. Since there is a close relationship between poverty and lack of educational facilities, it was most often the children in economically-disadvantaged states that were academically and culturally disadvantaged.

Many years of struggle among members of Congress on the wisdom or desirability of federal aid to education culminated in 1965 with the passage of several laws. Each law carries within it a statement that "Nothing in this Act, or in any other Act, shall be construed to authorize any department, agency, officer, or employee of the United States to exer-

Monkmeyer

A Neighborhood Youth Corps worker in a prekindergarten program.

⑦ Percent of Population 25 Years and Older With Less Than 4 Years of High School, by State, 1960

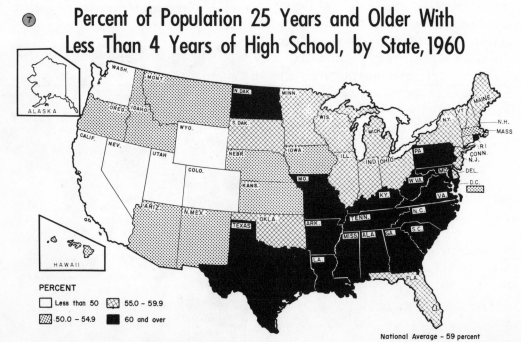

PERCENT

☐ Less than 50   ▨ 55.0 - 59.9

▨ 50.0 - 54.9   ■ 60 and over

National Average - 59 percent

Source: U.S. Department of Commerce, Bureau of the Census.

cise any direction, supervision, or control over the curriculum, program of instruction, administration, or personnel of any educational institution or over the selection of library resources."

By the year 1965 it was also possible to add the following provision to programs receiving federal funds: "No person in the United States shall, on the ground of race, color, or national origin, be excluded from participation in, be denied the benefits of, or be subject to discrimination under any program or activity receiving federal financial assistance."

Here are some of the education laws that are helping to equalize educational opportunity among young people in all states and territories of the United States:

The National Defense Education Act of 1958 to improve the teaching of science in elementary and secondary schools; to promote the teaching of mathematics and foreign languages to larger numbers of students.

Cooperative Research Program to study ways of improving the teaching of reading on the primary level; to help improve the education of teachers of blind students.

Higher Education Act of 1965 to extend college education. It provides that the university become a service agency for each community and authorizes colleges and universities to promote the training of leaders of social agencies, regional planning, engineering, and the like. Funds are provided to improve the library training and construction programs of colleges and to help small institutions to expand their services. Grants to students insure that every deserving high school graduate will be able to go to college.

The Elementary and Secondary Education Act of 1964 to help local school districts broaden and strengthen the quality of education offered by providing funds for equipment and materials; inservice education of teachers and supervisors; the use of school health, psychiatric, and psychological services; and many other provisions.

Economic Opportunity Act to provide funds for work-study programs and a second chance for school dropouts; Operation Head-Start for three and four-year-old children from impoverished homes.

Handicapped children are helped to become self-supporting citizens.
E. Bubley for Children's Bureau

Counseling a parent in the Community Action program.
Engelberg for OEO

Never Too Old To Learn

Adult class in fundamental education, Puerto Rico.

Classes for adults are not always held in school buildings. They may also be held in homes, outdoor areas, libraries; in factories, union halls, community centers, or in the armed forces. There are classes brought into the home or hospital by television or correspondence. This continuing interest in education is a good sign that people recognize the importance of education. An informed people is a strong bulwark for democracy against totalitarianism.

Training on the job.

About 30 million men and women in the nation are enrolled each year in some kinds of courses after working hours, during working hours, or between jobs. These are the people among us who have an ongoing interest in learning. They want to keep informed about current events in all fields of knowledge. They want to improve and upgrade their job skills. They want stimulating ways of spending their leisure time and retirement years.

American Indians attend school.

Adult class in typing.

The students in adult classes are recent arrivals who want to learn the American language and heritage. They are men and women who had little or no schooling as children because schools were not available. They are workers who seek to advance themselves to higher job opportunities. They are high school graduates eager for more education, though not necessarily studying for a degree. They are housewives who want to return to the business world. They are a growing army of men and women, and a welcome one.

For all of these people, now and in the future, there is an educational program offered by private agencies, public agencies, and industrial organizations. Federal assistance has become increasingly available to all.

A class in Rockingham, North Carolina.

91

The New Look in Schools

In order to keep pace with the tremendous amount of knowledge that must be passed along from one generation to another, schools must use the tools of technology. Look around in your classroom and school. Do you see a well-stocked library with microfilm, duplicating machines, and a wealth of reference materials? Are there science materials, tape recorders, filmstrip and movie projectors, overhead projectors, radio and television sets?

The devices are there to help you learn. But, just how does an individual really learn? This is the subject of unending research — the more the psychologists find out, the more they still need to learn. Teaching machines, according to some, hold the key. A teaching machine can be an inexpensive workbook-type course; or it can be a complicated computer-controlled machine like the experimental model shown here; or it can be a whole range of gadgets in between.

The most important aspect of a programed course is the skill of the programer in designing it to promote learning for each individual at his own pace. Here is how it works. A course is "programed" to give information in a step-by-step sequence. After each statement is made or principle explained, the learner tests his understanding by answering a question. If he answers correctly (by marking a paper or typing on a machine), he is directed to move forward. If he does not know the correct answer, he must turn to the section of the book or machine that gives additional help. In this way, step by step, each person learns — some quickly, and some at a slower rate.

The use of teaching machines is still limited because psychologists and teachers are still trying to find the best methods of learning a wide variety of subjects to suit the abilities of all learners. This much they all agree upon: machines will never replace the teacher. But, by encour-

Ford Foundation

Eastman Kodak

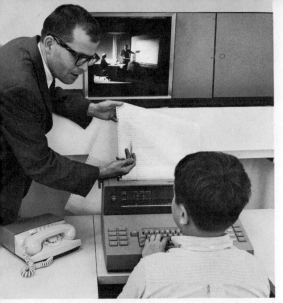

light. While this light is on, type your answer, then SIMULTANEOUSLY
depress the "ALTN CODING" and "3" keys.

      We are now prepared to help you learn a very quick method of squaring two digit
numbers that end in five (such as 35). However, we don't want to bore you by
presenting material you already know. Therefore, please answer the following
question. Do you already know a quick method of squaring numbers such as 45,
without using pencil and paper?

no

O.K. Let's learn it now then.
Do you know what the successor of a number is?
Answer yes or no.
no
When counting, the number which follows another is called the successor
of that number. Example: The successor of 3 is 4.
Question: The successor of 25 is ____.

26

Good.
The successor of 87 is ____.
88
Very good.
Eight times the successor of eight is ____.

72

Very good.

To square a two digit number ending in 5 we can:
    1. Multiply the leftmost digit by its successor.
    2. Write 25 after the result of Step 1.

EXAMPLE: The square of 25 is
    1. 2 times 3 (leftmost times successor) = 6.
    2. Write 25 after the product of Step 1 = 625.

IBM

IBM

aging students to learn independently, teachers will be able to give more time to individual guidance and group discussion.

The boy in this picture is taking a programed course that uses films and tape recordings at appropriate moments to elaborate on the information that comes from the computer. When the machine prints out a question, the boy types the answer and presses a button. Almost at once, the machine has a reaction to his reply, drawn from the storage unit where there is a collection of possible answers. If the student is correct, he is instructed to move ahead; if he is wrong, the machine gives him further instruction in informal language, somewhat as follows: "You are trying very hard, but think once more. What would you do if. . . . ." In fact, the learner soon forgets this is a robot teacher, so personal does the communication become.

Sheldon Equipment Co.

How Much Is Education Worth?

When Grandfather was a boy, anyone with an elementary school diploma could get a job, but the inexperienced worker had to wait several years and gain experience before he could expect to earn a better wage. An experienced worker had the advantage over the inexperienced one, regardless of the amount of education. Nowadays, it is considered more important to have an education than experience because a person with an adequate amount of schooling can be taught to meet the needs of a particular job. Job applicants today are expected to have at least a high school diploma, and, if possible, some college education.

IBM

Shipping room personnel need to be able to operate and understand computer equipment.

Modern living requires reading, writing, and problem solving.

USDA

94

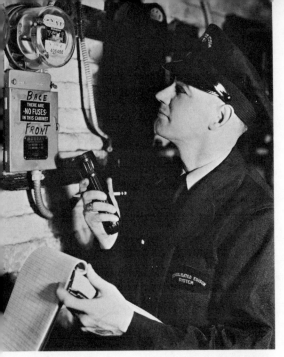

Other service jobs include meter reading. What skills does this man need?

Studies based on the earnings of workers show that an education does pay higher dividends. A worker with a high school diploma can expect to earn about $1,500 more a year than a man with 20 years of previous experience without such education. A college diploma can bring about $4,450 more a year.

The next time you become discouraged and want to quit school, look over the following figures:

Earnings as Related to Education

Age	Incomplete High School	High School Diploma	College Degree
14-24	$ 748	$2,469	$2,878
25-34	4,425	5,175	6,640
35-44	5,245	6,016	8,878
45-54	5,317	5,989	9,130
55-64	5,201	5,750	8,510

Based on 1960 U. S. Census figures

An adequate education is needed, not only for bread-and-butter reasons, but to equip the people to become intelligent and active homemakers, parents, citizens, consumers, and participants in sports, music, the arts, and travel.

Attendance at college is growing rapidly. In 1940, about 34% of the high school graduates went on to college. In 1965, the number of high school graduates doubled and the proportion that went to college increased to 54%. As the numbers rise, so will the prospects for a better job outlook.

A professional examination given to college graduates opens doors to various government agencies.

Clerical and professional workers are needed for jobs in government and private industry.

New Jobs Waiting

On the one hand we are told that thousands of workers are being displaced each year by new methods of production and distribution. On the other hand, there are long lists of jobs in the Help Wanted columns in all sections of the country. What does this mean to the young people now in school? Basically, it means that with an adequate education there need be no fear of unemployment.

There are and there always will be jobs for most of the work force of our nation. Large numbers of workers are needed to grow the food and other agricultural products, to produce processed foods, clothing, tools, and many other products. The great sums of money being spent in research laboratories by business and government lead to endless kinds of products, and eventually to new jobs. Compare the industries of today with those of a generation ago; look ahead to industries just on the horizon and you will see that the possibilities are limitless. Take the plastics industry as an example. Through continuing research by chemical engineers, formulas were found for molding, squeezing, laminating, casting, and rolling plastic substances into pipelines, auto bodies, fabrics, household utensils, mattresses, instruments for space vehicles, and so on and on. Hundreds of thousands of workers are needed to produce the raw materials as well as the wide variety of products made of plastic. The electronics, aerospace, food-processing, vending machine are just a few other industries that are developing new products and still newer industries. With a basic education, workers should have no difficulty in being trained for new jobs.

Most jobs of the future will be in the service and white-collar industries. These include jobs as repair men for telephone, electrical and electronic equipment; operators and mechanics for cars, buses, trucks, ships, and planes; chefs, nutritionists, barbers, beauticians, fashion designers, sales personnel; office workers and those who perform services in homes, hotels, laundries and cleaning establishments.

Among the white-collar jobs that will require at least a high school education and varying amounts of college training are health workers, secretaries, social workers, laboratory technicians. A college education will prepare men and women as teachers, accountants, lawyers, engineers, scientists, doctors, dentists, and many other professional workers in government and industry. One of the newest professional careers may be found in the data control industry. Before 1955 there were no workers in that industry; in 1965 there were 100,000 persons performing as programers, data analysts, computer engineers, and so on.

Employers give on-the-job training to applicants with a high school diploma, a professional certificate, or a college degree. This is in contrast to earlier requirements when schools had to train young people for particular job skills.

Enjoying Leisure

During most of history, man had to spend most of his working hours eking out a bare existence, beginning in childhood and continuing until old age. There was little time for recreation, culture, or hobbies.

With better working conditions, shorter work days, machines to do much of the hard work, and better wages, men and women now have time for activities that are not related to earning a living. People need to learn how to use this leisure time much as they need to learn how to perform their jobs. What can people do after work, during vacations, and in their retirement years?

The engineer, busy during his working hours with charts and measurements, finds the home carpentry shop an enjoyable hobby. Not so the carpenter. He seeks a change from carpentry and finds bowling with a group of friends his relaxation. The teacher looks forward to a Saturday game of golf, while the golf pro changes his routine to solving crossword puzzles.

There is always the quiet relaxation with one's family, discussing news events and watching a favorite television program. Many people have outdoor hobbies that may start with gardening and extend to birdwatching, rock collecting, sailing, hiking, or star gazing. Fortunately, there are still parks, foot paths, marshlands, and some wilderness areas where one can enjoy leisure during the changing seasons.

But leisure offers other bounties. It is a time to learn about so many things. Maybe it is reading about history from the dawn of time, or finding information about antique furniture, or how to assemble a solid-state radio. It may be learning a new language or skill. There are active sports as a game of golf, baseball, swimming; there are also spectator sports such as watching amateurs and professionals perform to the cheers and jeers of an audience.

The Arts In American Life

Audience of nearly 80,000 people listens to the New York Philharmonic Orchestra in Central Park, New York City.

The expression of human feelings and ideas is seen in a nation's art forms. Where there is freedom to create, there can be many artists; where there is freedom and a high standard of living, there can be wide audiences. Like education, the arts in America have been regarded as a community responsibility. But since communities have limited funds for such "frills," the arts are often left to chance, to commercial producers, and to the generosity of wealthy patrons.

Federal aid to the arts had a brief life-span during the depression years of the 1930's when the Works Progress Administration supported projects relating to dramatic and fine arts. These projects gave jobs to artists, sculptors, photographers, architects, and many other talented people who

to the fine arts

5c
U.S. POSTAGE

Award-winning design by Stuart-Davis, renowned artist, once a WPA instructor.

Above: Pablo Casals, master teacher.

Left: Cultural exchange — Galina Ulanova of the Bolshoi Ballet at an American performance.

could not find employment. There were opportunities in the dramatic, musical and dance arts for writers, directors, producers, and performers. They were able to contribute to a renewal of faith as people found diversion at little or no cost. Many of the artists have since become successful; many are now part of America's artistic heritage.

Large audiences are now available in all areas of the nation, seeking enjoyment in art museums and exhibits, symphony orchestras, ballet companies, and dramatic performances. A substantial public interest in FM radio, educational television, and "hi-fi" recordings has helped build a whole new industry.

Federal aid to the arts has been given through programs of the Smithsonian Institution which sends art and science exhibitions to colleges and supports theater groups in colleges. It also administers the Kennedy Center for the Performing Arts, in cooperation with the Metropolitan Opera Company. The Department of State arranges for cultural exchange with other nations.

In October 1965, Congress gave concrete expression to the need of the American people for a broader program in the arts when it established the National Academy of the Arts and Humanities. Funds were made available to help create nonprofit companies of drama, opera, and ballet, to support symphony orchestras, and give scholarships to artists. An American Film Institute will train promising craftsmen and performers for the film art.

The National Academy will assure the development of the arts. It will help people with creative talent to become self-supporting by serving appreciative audiences at moderate prices. What better use of public funds than to help people enjoy their leisure? The American people are at last in step with other, older nations who had, by tradition, supported national drama, opera, ballet, and concerts for many generations.

CHAPTER 5

EACH HUMAN BEING --
A VALUABLE RESOURCE

Ralph Waldo Emerson wrote in the mid-1800's, "The true test of a civilization is not the census, nor the size of cities, nor the crops — no, but the kind of man the country turns out." A society which has made the exploration of outer space an everyday activity has come to realize that the kind of people the country turns out is more important. In spite of great advances in technology and the highest standard of living in the world, there are still millions among us who are unable to share our great prosperity and abundance.

People who are poorly educated, unemployed, housed in slums, and deprived of civil rights in the conduct of their local and national affairs represent a grave social illness. To correct this illness has become a matter of national policy, and a great campaign is under way to build a better society through legislation, community action, self-help, and educational opportunities. This is one of the greatest programs of social improvement ever undertaken in a free nation. It is a further application of the principle set forth by the Founding Fathers that man has natural rights, such as life, liberty, and the pursuit of happiness; and that the government, deriving its just power from the consent of the governed, must assure these rights for all the people.

It is not only the poor who are under study in the great vision of the future. It is the right of children to be born healthy, of all people to be kept free of disease or cured when disease strikes, of aging people to be maintained in good physical and mental health, of the handicapped in body and mind to be cared for to the best of human knowledge and power — these are among the problems of human living that face generations now and in the future.

Who Are The Poor?

Rationing surplus food during the Great Depression, 1938, Cleveland, Ohio.

National Archives

In the 1930's there was a great world depression. A severe drop in production threw some 12 million people out of work in a short time. Almost everyone in the nation was economically deprived. Since that time, legislation and better planning on the part of the business community have almost eliminated the chance that such poverty would ever recur. For example, the President's Council of Economic Advisers tries to keep unemployment at or below 4% of the work force. If industry cannot find jobs for the unemployed above that figure, then government must be prepared to do so. In the generation following the Great Depression, unemployment rates have been kept fairly stable.

But during the 1960's it became clear that somehow "another America" had come into existence. According to Michael Harrington, author of a widely-read book, *The Other America*, there are between 40,000,000 and 50,000,000 Americans — approximately one-fourth of the population — living in poverty.

A family of four with an income of less than $3,000 annually is considered poor. An individual living on $1,500 per year is poor. If Harrington's figures are correct, then in this age of prosperity, *one out of four* of us is left out.

Can we put all employable persons into productive, income-producing activity while science and technology are abolishing the need for human assistance? Can our wealth and scientific know-how be used to abolish poverty as we increase our affluence? In times of depression, poverty is a temporary misfortune. In a stable and productive society, long-term and inherited poverty are serious matters.

Who are the poor in our era? The "new" poor are groups who were bypassed as the rest of society moved ahead. Poor farmers, migratory workers, and unorganized employees of hospitals, hotels, laundries, and service jobs are the "other Americans."

Whole communities and regions of the United States are pockets of

Can he move into the mainstream of American Society?

poverty. Thousands of miners who were displaced by machines are unable or unwilling to leave their home areas in what we call Appalachia. Although some of the more energetic and optimistic young people leave to seek opportunity in the cities, with limited skills and inadequate education their chances are not good. The people who remain behind are the defeated and the dispirited. Failure hangs like a choking cloud. New industries fail to move in where there is an inadequate labor force.

One-fourth of the total poor are the minority groups, mainly Negroes, Puerto Ricans, and Mexicans. They comprise the poor in the rural areas and towns. In large cities, the poor are those living in slum areas or in skid row where alcoholics, drifters, and other unattached homeless individuals assemble.

Millions of children are members of these poor families. According to the President's Council of Economic Advisers, about half of all these children are from broken families. Half of all the aged are poor.

Poverty costs the whole community a great deal. It certainly blights the lives and hopes of the millions who are its victims and robs them of the right to become constructive and creative members of society. Poverty also has serious and dangerous effects on those who are better off, and adds to the cost and problems resulting from crime, delinquency, and disease.

Since human beings are our most valuable resource, we should follow the advice of a great 12th century physician, Moses Ben Maimon, who wrote:

". . . . . Anticipate charity by preventing poverty; assist the reduced fellow man . . . . by teaching him a trade or putting him in a way of business, so that he may earn an honest livelihood and not be forced to the dreadful alternative of holding out his hand for charity."

A scene in skid row, any city.

The Poor Need More Than Money

The poor who inhabit the "other America" need more than money. Poverty cripples, and too often destroys, what is humane in man. We cannot end poverty by simply distributing money. We need to help individuals become proud and self-reliant members of a community. Unlike the people of other lands, no one in the United States starves or goes unclothed or unsheltered; yet we do have poverty, and a culture of poverty is a culture of despair, defeat, disease, and emotional disturbance. This culture exists in a number of "invisible" communities populated by millions who seem content to float, rather than swim, in the mainstream of American life.

More fortunate Americans have begun to realize that this group can

Volunteers (VISTA) help to guide the poor.
Engelberg for OEO

no longer be treated like economic lepers who need only be given handouts of food and clothing. In our society a person is valued and values himself on the basis of what he can contribute to the worth of the community, his world. The person who cannot make a meaningful contribution is deprived of an opportunity to build a basis for self-respect.

It is going to require many different programs and approaches to get these other Americans — often third or fourth-generation "other Americans" — into the larger American society. Programs have been put into operation in the fields of medicine, housing, education, mental health, rehabilitation of the handicapped, vocational training, urban redevelopment, and civil rights — all facets of what we call human resources.

In no single one of these areas can the massive problems of human wastage be solved. Serious, determined work on all fronts is needed to make it possible for poverty to be conquered in our time.

About 100 years ago, John Stuart Mill, an English political thinker, made the point that "the worth of a state, in the long run, is the worth of the individuals composing it. . . . . a state which dwarfs men in order that they may be more docile instruments in its hands, even for beneficial purposes, will find that with small men no great thing can be really accomplished."

Every anti-poverty activity is aimed at building individuals who are seen as priceless resources — to themselves as well as to the rest of society.

"I swear I begin to see the meaning
  of these things!
It is not the earth, it is not
  America, who is so great.
It is I who am great, or to be great
  it is you up there, or anyone;
It is to walk rapidly through
  civilizations, governments,
  theories;

Through poems, pageants, shows
  to form great individuals.
Underneath all, individuals!

"I swear nothing is good to me
  now that ignores individuals.
The American compact is
  altogether with individuals.
The only government is that which
  makes minute of individuals.
The whole theory of the universe
  is directed to one single
  individual.
Namely, to You."

       Walt Whitman (1819-1892)

107

Restoring A Region -- Appalachia

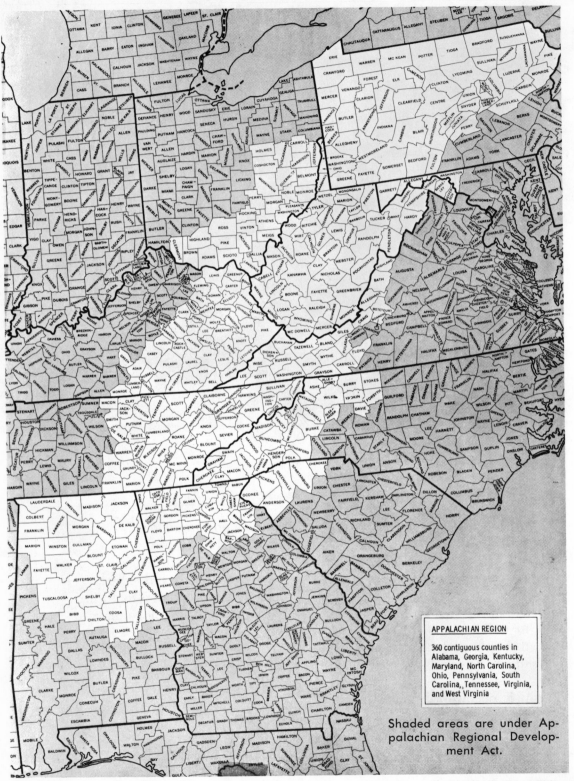

APPALACHIAN REGION

360 contiguous counties in Alabama, Georgia, Kentucky, Maryland, North Carolina, Ohio, Pennsylvania, South Carolina, Tennessee, Virginia, and West Virginia

Shaded areas are under Appalachian Regional Development Act.

Dept. of Health, Ed., & Welfare

108

The natives of Appalachia are the descendants of the pioneers who made their way over the dangerous Cumberland Gap some two hundred years ago. Although the coal deposits and other natural resources of the region have brought profit to many, the people of the area have been left behind. The poverty rate is extremely high; some 45% more than anywhere else in the nation receive public assistance. There are nearly 17 million men, women, and children in 360 counties of the states of Alabama, Georgia, Kentucky, Maryland, North Carolina, Ohio, Pennsylvania, South Carolina, Tennessee, Virginia, and West Virginia.

The governor of Maryland, concerned with the plight of the people, called a conference in 1960 of the governors of the states to find out what might be done to improve conditions. The recommendations of

Ford Foundation

A volunteer from one of the colleges helps tutor mountain children in North Carolina.

the Conference were presented to President Kennedy for consideration. After five years, Congress enacted the Appalachian Regional Development Act.

Appalachia today combines regional planning and local cooperation. The Appalachian Regional Commission recommends programs that should be carried out by each of the states. Among these are the construction of good roads to make the region accessible for tourism and business, the improvement of health and hospital facilities, and plans for housing, education, and vocational retraining. Farmers receive grants for soil and timber improvement on the land. Research is carried on to restore fish and wildlife habitat, perhaps in abandoned coal mines that have been filled in. Business firms are encouraged to set up industry throughout the region with grants in aid from the Commission. It is hoped that the people of Appalachia will become self-sustaining and productive once more.

A pencil factory brings employment opportunities to this region.

Ford Foundation

Childhood And Life Chances

Harold Liebow

"As the twig is bent so will the tree grow," goes an old saying. This applies to human beings as well as plants. No children enter school without previous experiences. Sometimes their parents have given them love, attention, playthings, folklore. This is not true for children of the "other America," the millions who grow up in poverty — children from broken homes, or in families whose yearly income is less than $3,000. Some of these children have never tasted an orange, used a pair of scissors, looked into a mirror, held a crayon, or used a toothbrush.

If a child comes from a large family that is also poor, he may be so shy and frightened that he has difficulty expressing himself. He has a limited and sparse vocabulary, never even speaking in complete sentences. When he starts school in the company of more fortunate children, he finds

Grete Mannheim

himself far behind and soon comes to feel frustrated. He starts a chain of defeat and failure through the grades and grows up with a negative attitude toward himself as a misfit, unless some serious effort is made very early in his life to break the chain of poverty.

Pre-school and nursery programs in which four-year-old children are encouraged to express their ideas and feelings, to play with others, and to handle many objects have been tried and found successful in many parts of the country.

It has been assumed for a long time that there is a close relationship between intelligence of children (as measured by the Intelligence Quotient) and the amount of reading, education, and cultural interests of the parents. In 1962, some investigators at the University of Rhode Island tested the hypothesis that children of high and low native intelligence could be differentiated by interviewing their mothers. Parents were questioned to find out the amount of intellectual stimulation that existed in the home. The interviewers predicted the IQ scores of 25 pre-school children (high or low) based on interviews with the parents, and their predictions proved correct.

Even though one cannot generalize on the basis of a study of 25 chil-

Engelberg for OEO

dren, studies of this type point to the need for a home life where there are stimulating learning environments for children from an early age. Where poverty, ignorance, or family disorganization may hinder a child's will to learn, it is the place of society to help improve the conditions.

If each community does not want to pay for the support of new generations of adult delinquents and educational cripples, it must get to the children during the early years. Society must provide the means by which each individual can be guided into a lifelong path of self-dependence and growth in learning. Playgrounds, supervised play areas, child care centers, and nursery schools are a good beginning.

Ford Foundation

111

Raising Aspirations

Children such as these can become self-respecting adults.   Engelberg for OEO

Young people who are motivated in childhood by parents who set standards of excellence will set goals for themselves that involve education and self-fulfillment. But what of the children who, after generations of poverty, have little desire to care and to believe in a personal future that includes an adequate education, occupational competence, independence, and self respect? For such children the problem is more complex than providing simple training in technical skills. How can the angry, defeated individual acquire a positive, optimistic view of himself and his life prospects?

In a study at Harvard University, psychologists sought to find out if the level of achievement of junior high school boys could be raised. The psychologists worked with young people along three main lines. First, they asked delinquent boys to speak into a tape recorder and paid them for their cooperation. The boys talked about themselves, their activities, dreams, hopes, grievances. Over a period of months, the boys had lots of opportunity to talk and to listen to themselves. They began to think of themselves less as undesirable and hopeless rejects and found positive ways of behaving.

The boys began to believe that they could change, and they did. First, in order to change their delinquent ways of behaving, it was necessary to improve their way of thinking about themselves. In the second phase of the study, a successful model was brought in — someone who had once been like themselves and had made a successful adjustment. This helped the young people to raise their levels of aspiration because they had seen and respected s o m e o n e who had successfully climbed to "higher ground."

In the third phase of the study, the boys worked in groups. They planned and carried out their own activities or followed a course of study. For example, the boys carried out their own safe-driving campaign and became interested in learnings that related to that project. Because the problem was theirs, and not imposed from the outside, the boys had a positive attitude toward learning.

Professor David McClelland, who carried out the study, recommended that there be a "new approach to educational programs for displaced workers (or under-achieving high school students) — an approach that concentrates on motivating the individuals to change their self-image, to dream up new possibilities for themselves, and then decide on and try out new courses of action which will certainly include new learning skills to fit the new self-image." To paraphrase an old adage, "You can lead a man to knowledge, but you can't make him learn." You had better concentrate on making him want to learn first.

Adolescents discuss their future chances.   Ford Foundation

Salvaging Our Youth

Ford Foundation

Student teacher works with young people, Kentucky.

In 1965, about 3,750,000, one of twenty persons in the total labor force, were unemployed. Among youth around the ages of 18 and 19, unemployment was even greater. In this group about one of six was out of work. Some two million young people come into the labor market each year. They are the children born in the years immediately after World War II. Of their number, three out of ten are school dropouts with little prospect of becoming self-supporting and productive adults.

Another group of young people are individuals between 16 and 21 who are not in school; nor are they even looking for work. They consist of about 200,000 young men and women.

What does this mean in terms of human resources? Why is it important that these young people be helped to become producers and consumers, and participating citizens in American society? What can be done for them that has not already been done?

Many programs are under way in each community to find out how these dislocated young people can be helped. Three programs operating throughout the nation have been given federal assistance.

The *Job Corps* is a program of remedial education and job-training for unemployed young men and women 16 through 21 years of age. The enrollees live, work, and learn in training centers located in cities as well as in rural areas. Applicants are sought through neighborhood publicity, assisted by thousands of volunteers.

The young people in the Corps are the uneducated who have the potential and the desire to break out of their poverty situation. Those selected are given a three-sided program of a) education, to make up for what the student has failed to achieve in school; b) job training, built around the Corpsman's aptitudes and the kinds of jobs in demand; c) physical development, including athletics, exercise, medical-dental care, and proper nutrition. Social experiences in the centers include various forms of recreation and opportunities for friendship and good sportsmanship.

Job training programs are guided by the Bureau of Labor Statistics which projects the occupations America will need for the next 10 years. For example, there is a need for thousands of typists, health assistants, nurse's aides, sales clerks, appliance repairmen, and automobile mechanics. Business firms offer jobs to Corps "graduates;" among them are automobile manufacturers, retail sales chain stores, and others.

The Job Corps enrollees will probably average a year of education, work, and physical training. They receive a small monthly allotment for incidental expenses and when they graduate they receive $50 for every month in the service. After the program, some of these young people may go on to receive on-the-job training in business, or they may decide to return to school. In this way, underprivileged youth are receiving a second chance.

The Neighborhood Youth Corps creates full or part-time jobs in the home area for those who want to remain in school. The trainees learn to operate duplicating or other office machines, tend switchboards, keep inventory records in a stockroom, assist with equipment in a laboratory or hospital. These part-time jobs do not add up to a career but they provide entry jobs with public agencies and nonprofit private firms. The beginning worker earns an income and,

of more value, he or she learns the habits and attitudes necessary for achievement in the world of work.

The *Work-Study Program* enables college students from low-income families to continue their studies. Students are given jobs as tutors, youth club leaders, recreation workers, and community service aides. The chief purpose of the program is to help every qualified high school graduate to enter and stay in college, regardless of the economic status of his family. Colleges now actually seek out poor but capable high school graduates and encourage them to enroll.

All of these programs work in close cooperation with other agencies, such as the local employment centers, Manpower Development and Training offices, the Department of Agriculture, and business firms to guide the young people along their way.

The money allocated to raise the living standard of the nation's poor is 1½ per cent of the annual federal budget, and only one-fourth of one per cent of the Gross National Product (the total income of the American people.) Does this not seem little enough to spend for so far-reaching a plan?

Neighborhood Youth Corps.

Engelberg for OEO

115

Our Aging Population

USDA

See what I made!

During prehistoric times people are thought to have lived an average of about 18 years in a lifetime. This was largely because a high percentage of individuals never survived infancy. During the time of the Roman Empire, life expectancy had risen to between 25 and 30 years. Now the average length of life for the world as a whole is about 45 years. In the advanced countries of Europe and North America, a child born today may expect to live to 75 years of age.

Increasing the life span is one of the great achievements of medical science, but it also means that in the future there will be a much higher proportion of older people. Between 1900 and 1950, for example, the number of persons aged 65 or over in the United States almost quadrupled — from 3 million to more than 11 million. By 1980 we will have about 20 million, and in the year 2,000 A.D. there should be well over 31 million oldsters. As a result of the increasing life span, our older population increases at a faster rate than the general population.

An aging population, though desirable, presents new problems and challenges. Scientists believe that if the individual can be protected from disease, a normal life span might even extend to 115 to 125 years! But, as people reach old age, they become less self-sustaining. What can be done to help them enjoy a happy and healthful maturity?

Programs such as Social Security, Old Age and Survivors Insurance, Medicare, and various forms of personal insurance and pensions deal with financial and health security. But the problems are more than physical and financial alone. There are psychological problems associated with aging which are now being studied along with the medical, social, and economic ones.

Population profile points up the increase of children and the elderly.

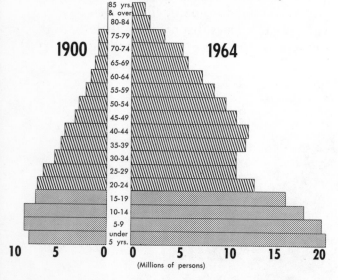

Chart of age distribution.

Research conducted under private and government auspices attempts to answer such questions as the following:

What is the aging process as it takes place in the cells and tissues of the body?

How do various parts of the body age?

Is there a relationship between aging and such serious diseases as cancer, arthritis, and heart disease?

How does aging affect general living and working?

Is there a decrease in the thinking powers of the older adult?

What changes in the heart muscle and blood vessels are caused by aging?

What are the differences in aging among the well-to-do as compared with poor individuals?

How do the attitudes of society and of the younger generation affect the mental health of aging individuals?

What can families, industry, and the community-at-large do to help?

These are some of the problems on which many young people now at school may work some day. The possibilities are intriguing for helping experienced, skilled, and mature people to apply the wisdom of years of living. People at any age need to feel respected and wanted, and old age is no exception.

There are programs of job opportunities in special workshops where unemployed senior citizens feel competent, worthy, and part of a group. There are housing programs built with older people in mind. At one

Neighbors in a housing project for senior citizens.

such development, built by the National Institute of Mental Health, the tenants are able to participate in educational, recreational, and social activities in a small community. Doctors and counselors are available to provide necessary services and advice. The results have yielded great satisfaction among the people, giving them a healthy self-concept.

When we show an interest in the problems and prospects of aging, we are really working for our own welfare. Each of us will some day be confronted with aging parents. All of us can look forward to growing old ourselves. What we accomplish now to enrich the quality and meaning of life for older citizens will reap benefits in our own golden years.

A study of nutrition in chronic illness in the aged, Duke University

Science Studies And Serves Man

Having performed unbelievable miracles in the research, development, and production of material goods, our nation is now committed to doing equally well in exploring how our human resources can be developed. Scientists reason that every event has a cause. Scientists interested in animal and human behavior (psychologists, sociologists, health workers) take the attitude that human behavior could be better understood if we could find out the causes of creativity, generosity, mental inadequacy, or delinquency. We would be able to take steps to create conditions that might improve desirable human behavior and eliminate anti-social behavior. New programs now under way or in planning are intended to upgrade and refine human resources and to improve living conditions by applying new knowledge about man. This new knowledge has been growing rapidly as a result of research in the behavioral and biological sciences.

One way of learning how the "inner space" of the human being works is to follow an individual through his life cycle — from the period before his birth throughout his lifetime. Studies are being made on all aspects of child health and human development. These studies coordinate all the fields of knowledge that relate to human life — the relation of man to the animal kingdom, and the interdependence of physical, chemical, mental and psychological conditions within the human body.

In 1963, a National Institute of Child Health and Development was established as an arm of the United States Public Health Service. It differs from earlier agencies in that it focuses attention on the complex health problems of the whole person, rather than on a single disease or body part. It seeks to search out the mysteries of the processes of biological as well as behavioral growth and development throughout the life span.

Children participating in a child study project. Boston Children's Hospital Medical Center.

Robert Howard for Boston Advertiser.

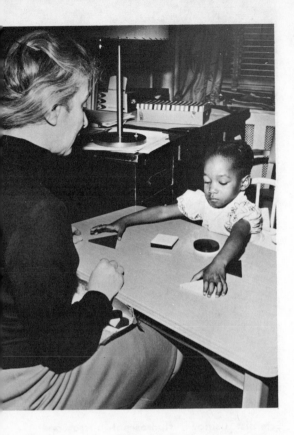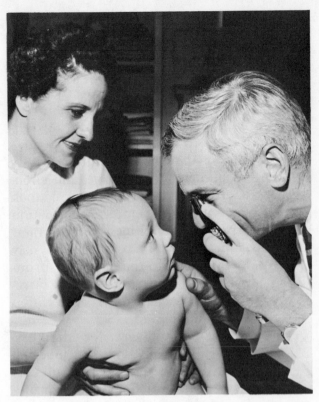

Mental and social development are studied, together with physical growth.

The Institute supports programs of training and research that deal with reproductive biology, prenatal biology, growth and development, aging, mental retardation, birth defects and developmental pharmacology (effect of drugs on birth).

Medical knowledge is being accumulated so rapidly that no one person can be expected to master all the information that bears on human development — aging, mental retardation, or human communication. Research in mental retardation, for example, uses the combined knowledge of biochemists, psychologists, surgeons, geneticists (who study the effect of genes on heredity), educators, biostatisticians, dietitions, hematologists (specialists in blood chemistry), and many other scientists.

Research scientists must apply what has been learned in fields of specialization outside of their own. A dentist uses supersonic energy to drill teeth; a surgeon uses electronic devices to "see" things inside the body that X-rays do not show; whole blood is quick-frozen and preserved; miniature, battery-operated devices are implanted under the skin; and a weakened or irregular heart is brought back to normal functioning. These are a few examples of how biology, medicine, engineering, and physics are coordinated as biomedical engineering. This gives some hint of how man and his problems are becoming the concern of scientists, engineers, and philosophers — how all science is, in a large sense, human science.

Chemistry And Human Behavior

Modern scientists are looking at the human organism as a complex system which is a combination of a number of smaller interacting subsystems. They are beginning to move beyond the consideration and study of the nervous, digestive, and circulatory functions of the body and look upon man as a complex information processing machine. From their point of view, human behavior may be compared to the output or printout of a computer which acts in response to specific input (education and training).

Man's equipment for thinking, feeling, learning, and remembering is based in the human brain and nervous system which operate with biological, chemical, and electrical assistance (described on page 76-7). Over sixty years ago, a British scientist predicted that some day we would discover the nature of the chemical substances that regulate the functioning of the human body. We would then be able to acquire complete control over the workings of the human body. This prediction is now almost a reality.

Pharmacology, one of the newer sciences, is concerned with the effects of biochemical processes and changes on human behavior. Extreme fatigue, for example, is known to result from the buildup in the blood of certain toxins (mildly poisonous chemicals) which force us to sleep or rest in order to restore a normal chemical balance. When a particular enzyme is missing at birth,

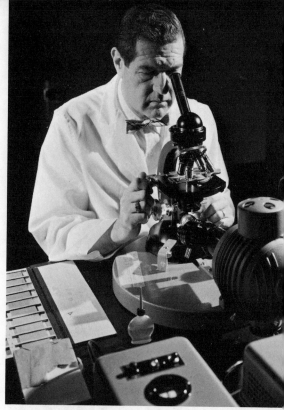

U. S. Public Health Service

Scientist using a fluorescent microscope to study biochemistry.

a condition known as phenylketonuria (PKU) is present. This results in mental retardation and it is now known that certain forms of abnormal development and behavior are the result of a biochemical "lesion" or break. The removal of PKU from the diet reduces mental malfunctioning. From such findings there is some hope that improvements will be made in the biochemistry of the brain.

During learning, there are changes in the electrical responses of the brain. Many different parts of the brain participate in learning. In cases of brain damage, if there is not too much destruction, an undamaged portion may take over and do the work formerly done by the destroyed part. Tiny electrodes may be placed inside the brain to help an individual make up for damage to important brain areas. This has been attempted with partial success.

The reason for differences in intelligence has long puzzled scientists. These differences may be the result of the way certain enzyme systems affect nervous excitability. Enzymes are a combination of substances which promote necessary chemical reactions within an organism. Certain other substances, such as small amounts of strychnine, if administered before an experience, can improve the rate of learning. Another substance, serotinin, if present in large concentrations, has been found to interfere with learning.

Laboratory experiments have compared the ability of bright and dull rats in learning to run through a maze. The proper dose of certain "learning" substances enabled the dull rats to learn as fast and perform as well as the brighter ones. Exactly how these substances affect the electricity and chemistry of the brain is not known. What is known is that they change the concentration of potassium and calcium.

These experiments point the way toward helping mentally retarded persons to learn new subjects or new skills. A new memory drug being tested on humans acts to speed up the production of RNA (ribonucleic acid) within the body. RNA has been found to be the key substance in memory and learning. If this new drug works as well with human subjects as it did in the animal laboratory, it may help raise intelligence and increase achievement for individuals at all levels of society.

What does this type of research predict for the future of man? We may be moving to a new stage of development in which the emphasis would move from attempting to control the environment to controlling and improving the physical and mental conditions of the human species. The result of this change may greatly reduce the number of persons confined to mental hospitals.

Computer-assisted research on the chemistry of the blood, University of California, Los Angeles.

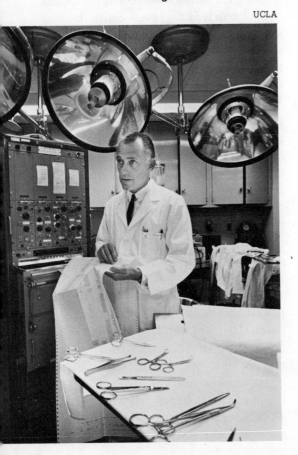

Closing The Health Gap

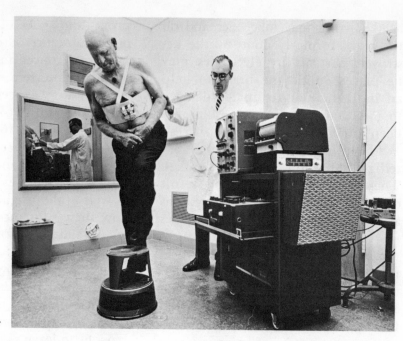

The heart action shown on the electro-cardiogram is radioed to a tape recorder, requiring no wire attachments.

Duke University

Far too many Americans are still trapped by illness. Present-day medical knowledge should make it possible for us to control heart disease, cancer, stroke, and other major causes of early death. Health programs are aimed at providing the services and resources that are necessary to meet the health needs of all our people. It is fairly obvious that widespread illness or fear of the costs of illness can hamper progress in other areas of life.

Many major health measures, enacted during the first session of the 89th Congress extended the chances for improving the health of all the people. These included: better health care of the aged; support for medical and other health-related professional schools; improved treatment for physical and mental illness; expanded efforts to reduce and eliminate air and water pollution.

In 1950, a total of about half-a-billion dollars was spent on public and private health research in the United States. Ten years later four times that amount was allotted, and the knowledge thus gained was spread among all the people. It may soon be possible to provide artificial hearts or other internal organs where the human organs are beyond repair. New discoveries open the way to new problems and new challenges. Biomedical engineering and other forms of research will help to combat disease and physical disability on a scale previously unattainable. This means, too, the continuing training of doctors and the establishment in all states of hospitals and health centers equipped to apply the most recent findings.

Medical research has greatly reduced the death rate from many diseases. In 1900, the five greatest killer diseases were, in rank order: pneumonia and influenza, tuberculosis, heart, cancer, and diphtheria. Today the order is heart, cancer, stroke, pneumonia and influenza, and hardening of the arteries. The diseases brought on by germs have been brought under control through knowledge and the use of vaccination and drugs. But doctors and biomedical scientists are now studying diseases that most often attack people in middle and old age.

The National Institutes of Health, the American Cancer Society, the American Heart Association, and many other research institutions and agencies use an increasingly complicated array of equipment in the diagnosis and treatment of disease. For example, patients with faulty hearts are now treated by surgery in remarkable ways. A heart-lung machine may be used to pump blood during a heart operation. Some heart patients are equipped with artificial valves of plastic or steel. Thousands of persons now live with a battery-operated pacemaker, a device that regulates the heart-beat. The battery is replaced by surgery every two or three years. The Atomic Energy Commission is sponsoring research to find a nuclear-powered pacemaker that will have a life span of ten years. Of course, the most spectacular development in heart research is the artificial heart, such as the one shown here, that can bypass a defective organ by pumping blood through the body.

Advances are being made each day in research on other circulatory diseases, stroke, cancer, arthritis, and mental disorders. There is still a great deal to be done.

Man's health goes beyond the structure and function of the body. His very survival may depend upon the purity of his environment, the air, water, and soil around him. These can no longer be taken for granted. From man's own carelessness in protecting his environment, he may make himself an endangered

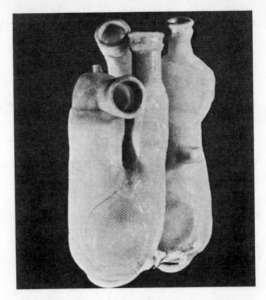

Model of an artificial heart pump.

species on earth with rivers choked with tons of floating dead fish destroyed by polluted water; shrimp and oyster populations dying; migrating birds with no nesting or feeding places; and people living in large cities where the air is polluted with harmful quantities of exhaust gases.

To improve such conditions, there are research and training programs dealing with air and water purification. The Water Pollution Control Administration has set up a demonstration program in river basins and watershed areas to show what techniques can be used to insure clean water throughout a region.

Thus, to close the health gap means much more than training doctors and finding new cures and vaccines. It is becoming clear that, if the human species is to survive, we must somehow create and preserve a total environment to promote good health. Perhaps we need a new group of health professions — those related to physical and mental health, as well as those that study, teach and prescribe for the total environment.

Power And Population On A Shrinking Planet

The new frontiers in this, the last third of the 20th century, are related to the conservation of human resources. Research and action programs are needed at every stage of human development from before birth to old age. No longer can the urban planners work apart from the sociologists, nor can the physical scientists separate themselves from the social scientists.

At a Congressional hearing, Dr. Roger Revelle, an oceanographer, urged more support to the sciences that deal directly with the problems of human beings. He said that this was our only hope if we are to deal with the problems rising out of the uses of technology and physical science. Dr. Revelle spoke also as director of the Center of Population Studies of Harvard University. He listed six major revolutions now in progress that hold either grave danger or great benefit for all of mankind.

There is a revolution in medicine and public health which has reduced the death rate, increased the life span, and increased the population.

There is a military revolution which has produced a "balance of terror." No one can hope to "win" a nuclear war.

There is an information and knowledge revolution aided and expanded by the development of computer technology. This places great power in the hands of large organizations, including governments.

There is a revolution in agriculture which enables a small percentage of the population to nourish the growing urban population of our own and other countries. Some 70 per cent of the people of the United States live in cities.

There is a revolution in the means of transportation and communication, bringing nations closer together and making the world's disadvantaged people aware of their needs and more demanding of immediate satisfaction.

There is a revolution in how man uses the natural resources of his environment with the aid of science and technology — reclaiming deserts, finding new uses for common minerals — and creating new problems associated with pollution of air, water, and soil.

All of these are major revolutions resulting from man's inventive genius. Now they demand thought and study to make sure that the end products are used to benefit man and society, and not to destroy them.

New methods of communication and education.

RCA

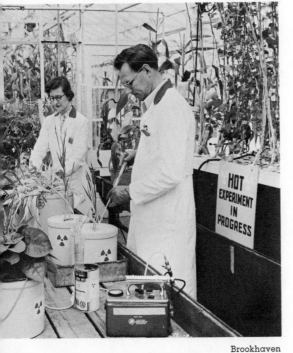

Brookhaven

Studying plant growth with radioactive isotopes.

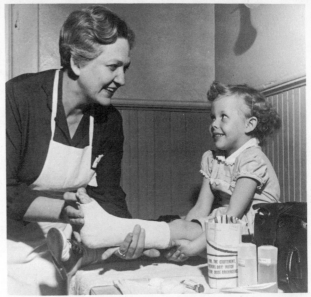

National Institutes of Health

Greater concern for public health.

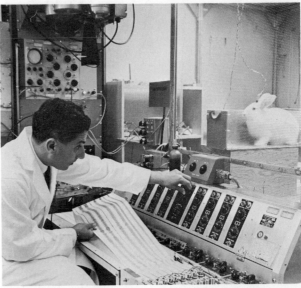

Ford Foundation

Research on population and fertility.

North Am. Aviation

But greater danger to the world's population from weapons of mass destruction.

United Nations

CHAPTER 6

HUMAN RESOURCES AROUND THE GLOBE

Nowadays some people would like to stop the world so that they could get off. Too much seems to be happening in too many places. It is difficult to see a clear pattern. It is not change alone that is upsetting us (the world has always been changing), but it is the speed of change. At the end of the last chapter, we spoke of six revolutions taking place in the American society. The word revolution has become a key word in modern speech, and not without justification. Social analysts and students of world affairs tell us that we are also living through other, worldwide revolutions — all related to each other and having profound effects on every aspect of living.

A *scientific revolution, a weapons revolution, and a revolution of rising expectations,* piled upon one another, are shaking up the present and affecting the future of every inhabitant of this planet. The challenges are worldwide and our actions must be broad enough to meet the challenges.

Let's look at the Science Revolution. The planet earth has been shrunk so much that there are no longer faraway places. A diplomatic conference may be convened within 24 hours, summoning delegates from all continents. A weather satellite makes continuous reports of weather conditions around the world, orbiting the planet every 90 minutes. A nomad in the Arabian desert listens by transistor radio to the same folk singers as people in Chicago. Television viewers of the United States, Canada, Latin America, and Europe may witness a space picture of the moon, a scientific encampment in Antarctica, a Congressional hearing, a United Nations conference, or the coronation of a monarch.

The Science Revolution has brought all people face to face with one another. There can no longer be any doubt that "all men are brothers." But the scientific advances seem to be moving us in two directions at once, and we have reached a fork in the road. Will it be science for abundance or for self-destruction? For the first time in history it may be possible — and it is, in fact, urgent — that all people everywhere help to provide a decent standard of living for those people who are poor. Yet, there is also the great reality that among the achievements of science and technology are deadly weapons of destruction.

The same science that can turn dirt into uranium and light beams into surgical instruments is responsible for the Weapons Revolution. The atomic weapon dropped on Japan in 1945 destroyed 100,000 human lives. The weapons that have been invented since that time could cost us half our population in the first few hours of combat! The major political powers have at their disposal atomic arsenals that could wipe out all human life on our planet. A world atomic war could begin and end within a few hours.

The very atom that was harnessed for weapons of destruction has been put to peaceful uses, too. Atomic energy now powers ships, provides electricity, and treats cancer. What becomes obvious as we think about the problem is not that it involves the bomb or even the scientist. The problem is still what it has been since our ancestors used rocks as both tools and weapons. The problem lies within man.

People in all parts of the world know now what takes place in other places. Television, radio, movies, newspapers in hundreds of languages communicate the activities of mankind. There is greater opportunity for personal contacts and friendship through trade, industry, diplomacy, and a great interest in world travel. Two billion people in the underdeveloped world no longer accept meekly the traditional conditions of starvation, squalor, disease, unemployment, exploitation, and ignorance.

Those people now see some hope for the future in which their own culture may be enriched by knowledge and new techniques. They look forward to the conquest of poverty and disease; they are demanding that what is known and possessed anywhere that can improve the human condition should be shared everywhere. They have seen the 20th century and they are impatient to take their place in it. This yearning, this aspiration, this new dynamic awareness is what has been named The Revolution of Rising Expectations.

Plans and programs that create conditions of peace, that help all people to share in the world's abundance, that roll back ignorance, superstition, poverty, and disease are not old-fashioned expressions of charity or welfare. Unless we take serious measures to use science and technology to fulfill the rising expectations of mankind, we may indeed have to stop the world and get off!

Devastation of the city of Hiroshima after the atomic blast of 1945.
Official U. S. Air Force Photo

Education Can Lead The Way

Less than two centuries ago, Europeans looked upon North America as a great underdeveloped nation. There were great untapped resources when the first European settlers arrived. It was the development of knowledge and universal education that helped to make available the supplies of oil, coal, uranium, metals, and water power that would have been useless to an uninformed and backward nation. Now countries of Asia, Africa, and Latin America are aware that unless they provide training and education, their populations cannot harness their great untapped human and physical resources.

Denmark may be cited as an example of one of the tiniest countries of the world that used the power of education as a lever in raising its standard of living. Its natural resources are limited and its soil is inferior to that of many underdeveloped parts of the world. About 100 years ago, Denmark was an agricultural country that had to meet severe competition from larger agricultural nations. The Danes met the challenge and set about transforming their economy. They began to specialize in dairy farming, best suited to their kind of soil. They formed cooperatives and found markets in the heavily industrialized countries of Europe and the United States. They developed new production techniques and entire new organizations for marketing. Today, the Danish standard of living for all of its people ranks with that of the United States, Canada, Switzerland, and Sweden.

Highly skilled labor of an educated population help the economy of Denmark.

The application of knowledge is changing our world so rapidly that continents once called "backward" and "sleeping" have begun to hurdle centuries. A new and basic hunger has emerged — the hunger for knowledge.

The great transformation taking place in our own time among people may be compared to certain chemical reactions. Without the presence of tiny amounts of a third substance (which is not itself affected), basic changes or combinations of matter cannot be achieved. This third substance is known as a catalyst. Education is the catalytic agent in the great drive forward of twentieth century mankind.

At last it is recognized that ignorance and illiteracy on a large scale are a kind of enslavement. The less educated a person is, the more restricted is he to the narrow, familiar, starved environment in which he was born. The more uneducated people there are in a nation, the harder it is for that nation to achieve a decent living standard.

Danish Information Service

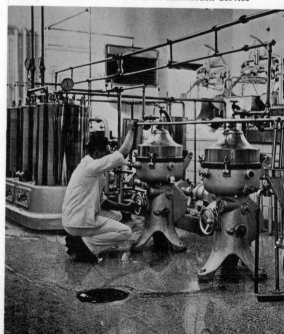

Teaching about nutrition to parents, Ghana.

Almasy for UNICEF

The campaign to reduce world illiteracy has been a concern of the United Nations Educational and Scientific Organization since its formation in 1948. Seven hundred million school-age children today are not, and have never been, in school. Great programs are under way with the cooperation of member governments to build schools and raise literacy levels. Other agencies of the United Nations provide technical assistance and support programs of education to help raise living standards. The Peace Corps volunteers who help set up schools in remote villages are acting as catalytic agents of the twentieth century.

Teachers, engineers, sanitation experts, missionaries, nutritionists, nurses, agronomists, craftsmen, doctors, communications specialists are all helping to wage a war against ignorance. Various specialized agencies of the United Nations and projects sponsored by individual governments, business organizations, philanthropic foundations are all cooperating.

Illiteracy, superstition, and backwardness are enemies that contribute to human degradation. The war front is everywhere on this planet and no one questions the rightness of the cause — or doubts the possibility of final and complete victory.

129

Food For A Hungry World

A great American philosopher said that man needs war, or a moral equivalent for war, because without being enlisted in some great cause man's existence does not seem to have much meaning. Another type of war in our times — in which all mankind should be involved — is the war against hunger. We, who live where many people are concerned with problems and illness resulting from overeating, may find it difficult to realize that starvation is right now facing most of the people of the world. Hunger and starvation exist on a scale the world has never known, mainly because there are larger populations in regions without the means of supporting them.

Here are a few facts. Malnutrition kills three million children every year. Hundreds of m i l l i o n s go through life stunted in heart, mind, and body because they never received proper amounts of proteins, minerals, and vitamins during their growing years. In underdeveloped countries, 75% of pre-school children suffer from some kind of malnutrition. Disease and hopelessness trap and cripple the underfed so that they neither care nor are capable of breaking out of their vicious conditions.

Unless we mobilize for war against hunger, the gap between food production and population growth will grow larger and millions more will face starvation than ever before in history. The reason can be explained as follows. It took man about 500,000 years to reach the present global population of 3 billion. Within only 35 years it is estimated that the number will reach between 6 and 7 billion. It took thousands of years to achieve the population figure of the present; it will take one generation to double it! Food supplies and food production are simply not keeping pace.

In the developed parts of the world, according to the Population Reference Bureau, agricultural production is a h e a d of population growth. In Africa and Latin America, population growth is outracing food production. In the underdeveloped regions, the amount of food produced per person has actually declined.

What can be done about this problem? What is being done? There are many programs under way. The nations that have reserves of food try to make the surplus available to the needy of other lands. This has been the policy of the United States

Food for Peace.

USDA

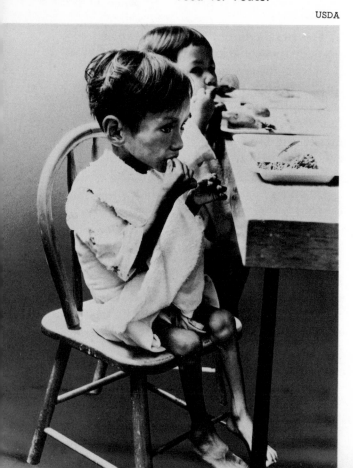

for several years. For example, it has provided half a million tons of grain per month to India's 480 million people over a period of years. So great is the crisis in that country that when the daily rice rations were cut from six ounces to a little more than four ounces per person, students and adults rioted in Kerala. Police and high government officials w e r e stoned and beaten. Buses were set afire and trains were stopped.

Sending f o o d surpluses to the world's needy is a humanitarian act, but this is a temporary solution. The excess food supplies are used up in a short time. If there is ever to be a "solution" or victory over hunger, other steps must be taken. There must be a rapid increase in food productivity throughout the world. Materials, equipment, and technical assistance can perform miracles leading to self-sufficiency. We must spread the knowledge gained by international scientists and engineers through irrigation projects, water control, fish farming, the use of fertilizers, hybrid seed, pesticides, and other aspects of modern farming. To these should be added land reform, mass education, greater access to farm machinery and supplies, and a rising purchasing power. These are the weapons to be deployed in the war against hunger.

Through the Food and Agriculture Organization, the United Nations is working around the clock around the world. Its work is supplemented by that of the World Health Organization, the United Nations International Children's Emergency Fund, and many other specialized agencies. The United Nations General Assembly in 1960 set a goal of 5 per cent increase in each developing country's income by 1970 in the "Decade of Development." T h i s would double the previous rate. "If we can achieve this," said Secretary-General U Thant, "the individual living standard can be doubled within 25 to 30 years."

Here are a few examples of how the United States has helped fight the world war against poverty. According to a Food for Peace Program, foods have been sent to India, Pakistan, and other famine-stricken lands. The East African republic of Somali was given help to establish a fishing fleet and a fish-freezing plant; in Nigeria, materials and equipment were sent to increase the supply of eggs and poultry through poultry farms; in the West Indian island of Jamaica, dairy farms were built to be operated by locally-trained farmers.

Population growth today is one of the gravest problems faced by all the nations of the world. When the matter was first discussed, leaders of some underdeveloped a r e a s complained that the "have" nations were trying to slow down the growth of the "have-not" world. T h e s e attitudes are changing as the underdeveloped nations recognize that a runaway population growth may wipe out their hoped-for development and a higher standard of living.

Specialists in many agencies of the United Nations are providing help to poor nations that are facing population control problems. The United States government has adopted a policy of making help in this field available to any nation that asks for it. No living species can reproduce itself unchecked indefinitely. Man has now to decide whether his species will bring itself under control or whether it will submit to the traditional checks of starvation, war, and disease.

Disease Is No Longer A Condition Of Life

There is an interesting theory that the great mystery of the rise and fall of civilization has more to do with microbes and insects than men. The anopheles mosquito, for example, has kept millions and millions of human beings weak and underdeveloped both individually and culturally.

The greatest conqueror the world has ever known, a young leader who blended the civilization of three continents — Africa, Asia, and Europe — was not felled in battle. He died in his early thirties of a malarial fever. His name was Alexander the Great.

Until the middle of this century malaria was the scourge of mankind. It shortened and destroyed more lives than any other disease. Americans became familiar with it when many of our soldiers contracted it during World War II in Asia and North Africa. (Within the United States, it had been completely stamped out early in the century after the source of the disease became known.) When the World Health Organization of the United Nations began to plan an attack on malaria, its germs were infecting 300 million people and killing three million of them annually.

Malaria is not transmitted directly from person to person. The cause is a parasite that is carried and nurtured in the stomach of the anopheles mosquito. This insect draws blood containing the parasite from one human being and then stings and infects others. A serious and fully-implemented drive to wipe out this carrier has been under way to lift the curse of the disease from the face of the earth forever. A weapon against the mosquito exists in DDT. After the female anopheles mosquito draws blood, she usually rests on a wall. If the wall has been sprayed with DDT, the contact will kill the mosquito.

Having learned how to combat the mosquito, teams have gone into action. In such widely scattered countries as Greece, Iraq, Nicaragua, Mexico, India, Borneo, Egypt, and Nigeria, spraying teams were sent out some twenty years ago. Every farmhouse, hut, market place, and houseboat was sprayed. Team members risked their lives to reach infested jungles and remote villages. As a result, the incidence of the disease has been greatly reduced and total victory is within sight. But — a new problem has arisen. New species of anopheles mosquitoes have emerged which are immune to DDT and, if they survive in large numbers, the disease cycle might start again. Scientists are working on a new approach. If the parasites that carry malaria can be killed off while they are in the human blood stream, the DDT-resistant mosquitoes could be rendered harmless. They might still sting and infect blood, but in the absence of the harmful parasites, their bite would be as harmless as that of other species of mosquito.

Ignorance, superstition, and tradition are often more stubborn enemies of health than disease germs. People do not readily give up traditional ways or the influence of village elders and witch doctors to accept scientific explanations.

The Population Dilemma

The sign of a nation's health and vigor is the rate of its population g r o w t h. The population of the United States grew 18.5% between 1950 and 1960 to a population of nearly 180 million. Many people were beginning to wonder about continued population growth. Demographers (those who study population trends) were beginning to warn that there are some disadvantages in "the more the merrier," when it comes to national census figures. Some alarmists even claimed that the growing threat of atomic bombs had even a greater potential enemy for world population. That enemy was the "population bomb."

Man has existed on earth for thousands of years. It is estimated that, when people began to live together

in settled communities about 10,000 years ago, there were about 10 million people on the entire planet. With limited food supplies and tremendous odds against survival beyond infancy, the population trend moved slowly upward. It took about 10,000 years for the world population to reach one billion — which was around 1850. But within 80 years (1930), that figure had doubled; and only 30 years later there were three billion people on earth. If the current rate of growth continues, within the lifetime of most readers of this page our planet will be the home of over seven billion persons!

This population trend is not even for all countries in all parts of the world. In general, the northern hemisphere countries that have much industry and high standards of living are increasing about half as fast as the underdeveloped areas of Asia, Africa, and Latin America.

Robert C. Cook, president of Population Reference Bureau, an organization that gathers and distributes information about population trends.

Ford Foundation

How would you interpret this estimate by United Nations experts for population increases between 1950 and 2000?

World population increase	4-1/2 billion
North American population increase	1/10 billion
Latin American population increase	1/2 billion
Asian population increase	2-9/10 billion

Another way of examining the prospect is to say that in the 50 years between 1950 and 2000, the increase in the population of Asia will be about equal to the entire world population in 1960. If we realize that a family with a limited income and a large number of children to feed, clothe, house, nurse, and educate must spread its resources thin, then it follows that a nation, too, faces similar problems. With great strides in medical science that have been applied throughout the world, there has been a sharp reduction in the world death rate, especially since World War II. Millions of children once died in infancy of communicable disease and faulty nutrition; today most of those survive, though many of them exist on a meager standard of living.

Large populations in poor countries present grave problems of raising e n o u g h food and providing homes, health services, education, and all the other needs of human existence. In the high-growth areas there is a large proportion of children and a much smaller proportion of adults in the productive working ages. For example, the population under age 15 in the underdeveloped countries is 45%; in the highly industrialized nations the child population is about 20%.

Entering The 20th Century

Tourists to all parts of the world are finding many familiar sights all mingled with the culture of the nations concerned. There is, for example, the development of colleges and training c e n t e r s for technicians. There are rapidly rising cities that crowd in the old and new in traffic, highways, high-rise office buildings, low-cost housing for the workers.

There are workers in the fields using modern equipment side by side with those still using the sickle and ox-drawn carts. There are factories producing goods for distant markets and craftsmen developing home industries.

Each nation is undergoing change in a thousand ways — and each nation adapts to the changes in its own way. This team in Sierra Leone, Africa is surveying the best uses of the land with technical assistance from the Food and Agriculture Organization. This region appears to be good for developing cocoa cultivation and processing.

The Nigerian government is developing its own corps of architects to help b u i l d public buildings, schools, playgrounds, and homes.

The newest media are used to leap the hurdle of centuries in conveying knowledge to the people. No longer is it necessary to wait until people can read and write; governments make use of motion pictures, radio and television to educate the people throughout the land on public matters and for self-government. The film projectionists come from the Stone Age tribal culture seen on page 11.

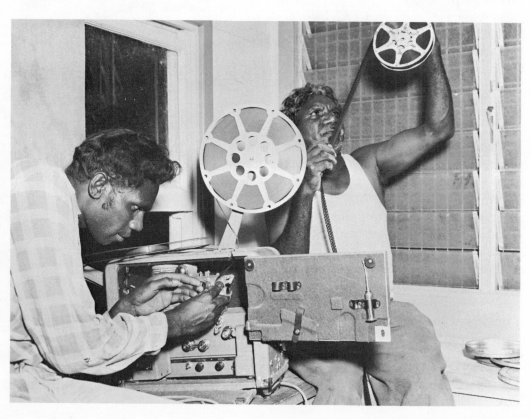

International Cooperation

United Nations

Men, societies, and nations since earliest times have cooperated with one another in some way. Even wars are short intervals between long periods of communication and the interchange of ideas, goods, and people. Early civilizations, as noted earlier in the book, did not spring up in complete isolation from each other. Ar-

chaeological evidence makes a very strong case for the spread of such important inventions as agriculture, record keeping, and metal working from their place of origin, Mesopotamia, to Egypt, India, and China.

The contacts and communication have been with us throughout history. The process of diffusion is still going on, but at electronic speeds. The big question for the 20th century is what should be the nature of our contacts with one another? Will we have conflict and decline, or cooperation and human betterment? From one point of view, we see the spread of nuclear weapons, population expansion, rising poverty, and accelerating social and technological change. But the forces that drive the human race toward unity and reason are also evident and b e c o m i n g stronger.

For example, 1965 was called the International Cooperation Year. At a conference in Washington, D.C.,

United Nations

5,000 Americans representing corporations, educational institutions, foundations, labor, and government assembled to involve the "best minds and boldest spirits in the quest for a new order of world cooperation." This was only one of many meetings that took place throughout the world under the ICY, the project proclaimed to celebrate the 20th anniversary of the United Nations.

Some eight years earlier, in 1957-1958, the world had seen another example of international cooperation. Through the International Geophysical Year, geographers and scientists from many lands shared research experiences and knowledge about the earth and its physical environment. The success of the IGY led to plans for a world endeavor which would involve people in planning for humanity.

Cooperation is only a word until we see just what it is that people are thinking and doing for their mutual benefit. "Since wars begin in the minds of men, it is in the minds of men that the defenses of peace must be constructed," states the preamble to the Constitution of the United Nations Educational, Scientific and Cultural Organization. That agency is publishing a series of volumes of a universal world history. Historians from many lands are attempting to agree on the interpretation of facts and ideas that will promote attitudes of peace and mutual respect instead of hostility and suspicion. Imagine the great contribution to international understanding if we had a universal world history which could be taught in American, British, Russian, Chinese, German, Egyptian, Israeli, African, or Latin American classrooms. This kind of study would emphasize similarities and help all people to appreciate differences, thereby taking a long step toward erasing war from the minds of men.

On another front, Chief Justice Warren of the United States Supreme Court reported on two world conferences of the legal profession which, he stated, "fortified my faith in mankind's capacity to develop international law into a major factor for world peace. More than a thousand law leaders from over 100 nations came to Athens (in 1963) and over 3,000 from some 115 nations gathered in Washington (in 1965) to hammer out the specifics of a work program to strengthen international law and international courts."

USDA

Food for Peace is distributed in Afghanistan through CARE, a voluntary American Agency.

Future Planning That Goes Beyond Political Boundaries

Standard Oil (N.J.)

Mekong River Development Area.

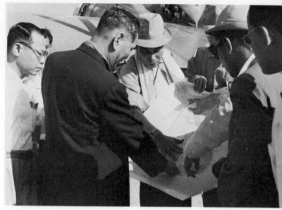

United Nations

A team of Japanese experts survey the river basin.

Civilization began and flourished around rivers, and man is still dependent upon water for agriculture, transportation, and power. The Mekong River in Southeast Asia is the lifeblood of four countries — Cambodia, Laos, Thailand, and South Vietnam. An independent agency of the United Nations, the Economic Commission for Asia and the Far East (ECAFE) has brought the four countries together — some of whom are technically at war with one another — to plan the development of the Mekong River Basin. It is no easy task to get four independent nations to agree on a project in which each may have to yield some of its power in order to benefit a larger region.

Each year in the lower delta basin there is a period of flooding during the monsoon season and a long period of drought. A long-range project to control the water's flow has been undertaken by 16 nations of the world assisted by the United Nations agencies, foundation grants, and business firms. Of the amount needed to complete this project, about one-third will come from the four nations involved and the rest from the nations of the world. For example, France sent funds to begin the surveys; India sent gauges; Israel and Taiwan sent cement; Iran shipped oil supplies. The Japanese sent experts to the area and invited local engineers to study how Japan has harnessed its rivers. There were surveyors, engineers, meteorologists from England, the Philippines, and the United States.

When completed, irrigation will double the cropland in an area about as large as France. Floods will be controlled and new lakes will help to improve navigation. There will be abundant electric power for farming and industry — all affecting the lives of 25 million people. One unique aspect of the Mekong River plan is that it includes the knowledge and experience of scientists and technologists, together with that of social scientists. Instead of a population crowded into rice paddy areas that depend on flood seasons, there will be greater variety and productivity in farming. Electricity will make possible processing and other industrial plants; together with improved shipping facilities, remote villages will become towns and cities.

Education is an integral part of the river development project because local farmers need to learn how to carry on modern farming methods on pilot experimental farms; villagers need to be trained as advisers to all the people coming in to build up the land, and an informed population will have the desire to build a new way of life.

One small dam, the Nam Pong in Thailand, was recently completed. The money for the dam ($25,000,-000) was loaned by West Germany to Thailand. The site had been surveyed by a Japanese firm. Construction was completed by a West German company. Overall planning was carried on by a committee of representatives of the four Mekong Valley countries under the direction of ECAFE with "seed money" from the United Nations Special Fund.

Engineers, geologists, agriculturists, and world planners are busy on other continents, too. In Latin America, plans are being drawn to extend the usefulness of the Paraguay River which flows through five countries and affects the people living in a million square miles. Instead of seasonal floods and the loss of great quantities of topsoil that clog harbors, the river will be used for irrigation, electric power, navigation, agricultural expansion, minerals, and ores.

International conferences and collaboration on water desalination and

A Cambodian technician uses equipment supplied by France.

the use of water resources are part of the International Hydrological Decade begun in 1965.

The Antarctic has been declared an international area for study under a 1959 treaty by which scientists from 24 countries pool findings that may affect the future food supply, communications system, and space achievements of all mankind.

Can you see that international cooperation is becoming inevitable in every field where man seeks to move ahead? Citizens of the 21st century will know much about the space race and the arms race; they will also be involved, as we are today, in solving the problems of and lifting the burdens from the human race.

A milestone in the Mekong River Project, the completed Ubol Ratana Dam in Thailand. Its power station will provide electric energy; the water will irrigate a large area of farmland.

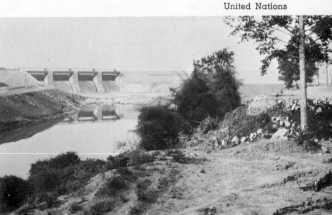

Glossary

Appalachia. A region extending through 11 states that has a high unemployment and poverty rate. Appalachian Regional Commission is carrying out programs to raise living standards.

Archaeology. The study of the remains of early cultures to determine how they lived.

Automation. The use of machines to drive and regulate other machines, thereby adding "thinking" to man's muscle power. Automation makes possible the great industrial development that exists in large areas of the world.

Behavioral Sciences. The study of how and why people behave as they do. Research in the medical, biological, and psychological sciences tries to note the interrelationship between the structure, chemistry, and function of the body in determining intelligence and human or animal behavior.

Biological Sciences. The study of living things through anatomy, physics, chemistry, and other related sciences.

Biomedical Engineering. The coordination of medicine with engineering to help improve body functioning, as through mechanical limbs, kidneys, heart pumps, etc.

Capitalism. The economic system under which we live, characterized by the individual ownership of goods, land, and business.

Civilization. The advanced form of culture, from the Latin word *civitas,* meaning city.

Culture. The things that are learned and passed on by people — language, customs, beliefs, arts, technology, etc.

Closed Society. The economic and social system which keeps a person within the level to which he was born, with rare opportunity for improving his status. Contrasts with the Open Society under which we live.

Computers. Machines that perform number operations by mechanical or electronic devices. They calculate, store, adjust, and record information at the speed of light. Computers have tremendously improved man's efficiency in the conduct of business and government.

Corporation. A business enterprise organized by selling shares of stock to individuals. The money thus invested is used to earn more money.

Data Processing. The recently-developed business technology that involves programing, analyzing, storing, and retrieving information through the use of computers.

Fertile Crescent. Area in the valley of the Nile River and the valley of the Tigris-Euphrates River in which civilization (cities, advanced forms of agriculture, trade, etc.) developed. Among the peoples of the area were the Egyptians, Babylonians, Sumerians, Hittites, Hebrews, and others. (See Index).

Government. A form of social and political organization that dates back to early man; it regulates how people can live and work together in groups.

Human Resources. The combined creative abilities inherent in the people of a nation.

Industrial Revolution. The period of cultural development that began in England at the beginning of the 18th century, when power-driven machines were invented to improve the quantity and quality of manufactured goods. The computer-assisted machine age now in process is sometimes called *The Second Industrial Revolution.*

Literacy. The ability of an individual to gain information by reading and to communicate information by writing. A society with a high degree of literacy among its people has a greater chance for industrial and scientific development than one where illiteracy is predominant. One of the goals of the global great society is to increase literacy.

Mass Production. The system for increasing productivity which uses machines and the division of labor. Each worker has a special job to do instead of producing the product by himself.

Mechanization. The addition of mechanical power to the production of goods — steam, water, electricity, etc. Mechanization adds power to human muscles, often imitating the steps traditionally used in production but greatly improving the quantity and quality of output.

Middle Ages. The period of history (11-14 century) when Greek, Roman, and other European cultures were nearly destroyed through war and conquest. In Asia, Africa, and the Western Hemisphere, however, cultures were thriving.

Millennium. A period of a thousand years in describing historical development. *mille,* Latin for thousand; *annus,* year.

Open Society. The economic and social system which, in contrast to the Closed Society permits citizens to move from one economic level to another — from poor man to rich man — on the basis of ability and opportunity.

Prehistoric Man. Tribes of people who lived before the time of written records, including Australopithecus africanus, Neanderthal Man, Pekin Man, Cro-Magnon Man. (See Index)

Purchasing Power. The amount of goods and services that the people of a nation can afford to buy with the income earned. Greater purchasing power makes for greater demand for consumer goods, thus greater employment and production.

The Reformation. A religious movement of protest against Catholicism, started in Germany in the 16th century by Martin Luther. Introduction of Protestant Christianity.

The Renaissance. Period of history, 14-16 centuries, that brought about a great revival of learning and creativity in Europe. Started in Italy and spread throughout the continent, marking the transition from medieval to modern history.

Specialization. Stage of human cultural development when individuals became skilled at trades, crafts, or arts and exchanged their abilities for food and other needs.

Standard of Living. The ability of the mass of people of a nation to buy capital goods and services. Industrialized nations, such as United States, Canada, Japan, countries of Europe, have a high standard of living; underdeveloped nations do not.

Technology. The aspect of human culture that deals with tools and machines in the production of goods.

Thermostat. One of the basic inventions of the automated age. It is an apparatus for automatically regulating temperature. A change in temperature causes the expansion or contraction of a metallic substance and causes a machine to stop or start.

Index